R.D. Laing and the Paths of Anti-Psychiatry

Zbigniew Kotowicz

ROUTLEDGE

London and New York

First published 1997
by Routledge
11 New Fetter Lane, London EC4P 4EE

Simultaneously published in the USA and Canada
by Routledge
29 West 35th Street, New York, NY 10001

© 1997 Zbigniew Kotowicz

Typeset in Times by LaserScript, Mitcham, Surrey
Printed and bound in Great Britain by Clays Ltd, St. Ives PLC

British Library Cataloguing in Publication Data
A catalogue record for this book is available from the British Library

Library of Congress Cataloging in Publication Data
Kotowicz, Zbigniew, 1950–
    R.D. Laing and the paths of anti-psychiatry/Zbigniew Kotowicz.
    p. cm. – (Makers of modern psychotherapy)
    Includes bibliographical references and index.
    1. Laing, R.D. (Ronald David), 1927–   . 2. Antipsychiatry.
    3. Psychiatry – Philosophy. I. Title. II. Series.
RC438.6.L34K68   1997
616.89′001 – dc20
                                                          96-32541
                                                               CIP

ISBN 0–415–11610–4 (hbk)
ISBN 0–415–11611–2 (pbk)

Thus it was necessary that every hour in the wards should increase, together with his esteem for the patients, his loathing of the textbook attitude towards them, the complacent scientific conceptualism that made contact with outer reality the index of mental well-being. Every hour did.

The nature of outer reality remained obscure. The men, women and children of science would seem to have as many ways of kneeling to their facts as any other body of illuminati. The definition of outer reality, or of reality short and simple, varied according to the sensibility of the definer. But all seemed agreed that contact with it, even the layman's muzzy contact, was a rare privilege.

On this basis the patients were described as 'cut off' from reality, from the rudimentary blessings of the layman's reality, if not altogether as in severer cases, then in certain fundamental respects. The function of treatment was to bridge the gulf, translate the sufferer from his own pernicious little private dungheap to the glorious world of discreet particles, where it would be his inestimable prerogative once again to wonder, love, hate, desire, rejoice and howl in a reasonable manner, and comfort himself with the society of others in the same predicament.

Samuel Beckett, *Murphy*

Contents

Acknowledgements

I would like to thank the following who have read parts or all of this text in its earlier stages and gave their helpful comments: Madelyn Brewer, Duncan Brewer, Aldous Eveleigh, John Heaton, Lucy King, Anthony Rudolf and Laurence Spurling. I would also like to thank Sabine Cornille, former lecturer at Paris VIII (Vincennes), for her help in preparing an account of the activities of Sozialistisches Patienten Kollektiv, as well as Professor Alec Jenner and David Hewison for supplying me with various bits of information about the patients' self-help groups.

Abbreviations

DS   *The Divided Self*
SO   *Self and Others*
RV   *Reason and Violence. A Decade of Sartre's Philosophy.*
        1950–1960
SMF   *Sanity, Madness and the Family*
IP   *Interpersonal Perception*
PE   *The Politics of Experience* and *The Bird of Paradise*
PF   *The Politics of the Family*
K   *Knots*
WMF   *Wisdom, Madness and Folly. The Making of a Psychiatrist*

(Publication details can be found in the Bibliography.)

Chapter 1

Introduction

I

It is rare for an intellectual to gain celebrity in such a short period as did Ronald D. Laing. And when this intellectual happens to be a psychiatrist then we are dealing with a very rare phenomenon indeed. His public presence was such that he became a household name. He was read widely by professionals and lay persons alike. Books were written about him, interviews with him were conducted and published, references to his works could be found everywhere. His works were almost immediately translated into major foreign languages and he became a voice heard throughout Europe and across the Atlantic.

Laing touched a raw nerve. To put it briefly, he attempted to politicize and spiritualize, so to speak, the discourse of madness and in the process, in a truly anarchic fashion, he questioned, doubted, ridiculed some of the fundamental precepts that govern our society. Laing sought passages between the so-called normal and the insane; he fervently believed that the language of madness is a human language and that it can only be understood if it is accepted as part of the human experience. Laing was the celebrated psychiatrist, the visionary, the savage iconoclast who questioned the values of the developing capitalist society in general and the role of psychiatry in particular. He attempted to bring madness back to the public space, where it once was, before it was separated off, incarcerated, confined in lunatic asylums on the outskirts of the great conglomerations where normal citizens conduct their daily affairs.

And then, just as quickly as he rose to prominence, Laing faded away. A generation later he is a distant, almost irrelevant figure, and he needs to be introduced anew. It is quite amazing to think that had he been alive he would be, at the time of writing these lines, only sixty-nine.

Laing was born on 7 October 1927 in Glasgow in a lower middle-class Presbyterian family. He was the only child. His upbringing and education were fairly conventional – primary school, grammar school, university. He studied medicine, specialized in neurology and psychiatry. At the end of his studies Laing had arranged to continue his education abroad under the guidance of the famous German psychiatrist and philosopher Karl Jaspers. But the authorities did not concur, the Korean War was on, the Army needed medically qualified staff and so, instead of going to Basel to work with Jaspers, Laing landed in a British Army psychiatric unit in the rank of corporal. After two years he moved on to work in a general psychiatric hospital and another two years later, at the age of twenty-eight, he became a senior registrar in the Psychiatry Unit of Glasgow University. After a further two years Laing took up a post at the Tavistock Clinic in London and began training as a psychoanalyst.[1]

The rise in the professional hierarchy was swift, one could almost say spectacular, but well within the established channels. The one distinguishing feature in Laing's career, up to this point, was his attempt to study under Jaspers. Quite unusually for someone educated at that time in Britain Laing felt drawn to the philosophical tradition of the Continent, chiefly phenomenology and existentialism. Most of the relevant writings were untranslated, they had the reputation of being obscure and were considered too far removed from the prevailing positivist stance of medicine and psychiatry. Shortly after settling in London Laing published his first book, *The Divided Self* (1960). This book signalled someone with a difference. On the one hand, *The Divided Self* is a straightforward monograph which brings close to the reader the experience of becoming schizophrenic; on the other hand, Laing puts all the clinical material within a framework made of categories derived from the existential thinkers. In the English-speaking culture a work of this kind was absolutely unique, almost alien. Despite this (because of this?) *The Divided Self* became in time a spectacular success.

At the Tavistock Clinic Laing began research into interpersonal interaction and patterns of family communication. Two publications – *Sanity, Madness and the Family* (1964) (with Aaron Esterson) and *Interpersonal Perception* (1966) (with H. Phillipson and A.R. Lee) – were reports on this research. Other works – *Self and Others* (1961), *Reason and Violence. A Decade of Sartre's Philosophy. 1950–1960* (1964) (with David Cooper), *The Politics of the Family* (1969), and *Knots* (1970) are theoretical writings in which Laing's vision of the interpersonal world comes through. This time, too, there was a large element of 'imported' thought, mostly coming from America, where research into family interactions had already been under way for quite a few years. Laing's writings on the subject usually have a hard edge. He greatly highlighted the psychological violence that goes on in families and went on to argue that within the context of these families madness is quite intelligible. In the more popular perception it appeared that Laing was accusing families of driving their children mad, although he never explicitly expressed this view.

In 1967 Laing brought out *The Politics of Experience* and *The Bird of Paradise*. In some respects this has been his most notorious work and it marked a complete break with the norms of the psychiatric orthodoxy. What distinguished *The Divided Self* was the unusual perspective from which Laing approached the subject of mental illness; *The Politics of Experience* presented the public with a completely reversed picture. Laing questioned the actual value system on which our notions of 'madness' and 'normality' is based. He argued that the 'mad' were sometimes more sane than the 'normal'. Moreover, Laing came to think that some psychotic experiences may have a healing dimension, akin to rituals of initiation, where through the loss of the sense of the ego and after a voyage into a mystical sphere a new, more enlightened person could emerge. *The Politics of Experience* elevated Laing into the realm of stardom and at the same time it divided public opinion. His first claim to fame had been that of a psychiatrist with a reputation for understanding the mentally ill and the family structures in which they grow up. After *The Politics of Experience* Laing came to be perceived as a maverick guru of schizophrenics, a leader of society's vanguard who, through experiences of transcendental reality, would break out of the vicious circle in which the modern capitalist society imprisons its citizens.

Another venture which increased Laing's fame was the Kingsley Hall therapeutic community, set up in 1965. This was an attempt to create conditions in which people going through a psychotic breakdown could overcome it in a non-medical environment. The patient/doctor structure was abolished, and all lived together under the same roof. Seminars and various workshops were held at Kingsley Hall and the place quickly became very famous. The community was part of the new counter-cultural scene in London and gossip of all manner about it circulated, adding to the aura that surrounded Laing.

In 1970 the five-year lease on Kingsley Hall came to an end. Laing took this as an opportunity to have a break. At the time he was becoming increasingly interested in Eastern religions and meditation and decided to go to the Orient. His destination was first a Buddhist monastery in Ceylon (now Sri Lanka) and then India. He was away for over a year.

After the return the pace slackened markedly. Laing was lecturing widely but no new substantial work was coming out. Also his interests seemed to go further and further away from psychiatry. For a period he took an interest in the birth techniques of Le Boyer. Out of this came *The Facts of Life* (1976), a collection of speculations about birth and pre-birth experience, some autobiographical reminiscences, and a scathing attack on the dehumanizing aspects of medicine. Over the next three years three slim volumes of very personal writings *Do You Love Me?* (1976), *Conversations with Children* (1977) and *Sonnets* (1979) appeared. These were literary efforts, little ditties and poems, as well as recordings of actual spontaneous conversations with children. The next 'serious' publication was *The Voice of Experience* (1982). The book has little to do with psychiatry. It is more a collection of observations on the mystery of it all, on mysticism, birth, out-of-body experiences and on the inadequacy of positivist science to deal with it. In 1985 Laing published a memoir *Wisdom, Madness and Folly*. The book covers Laing's childhood, school, university and first three appointments as a psychiatrist and breaks off at the end of his time in Glasgow. Four years later, on 23 August 1989, in St Tropez, Laing died of a heart attack during a game of tennis. He was apparently a very keen player.

II

Many of Laing's projects were collaborations with others. The studies of schizophrenic families in *Sanity, Madness and the Family* were done together with Aaron Esterson; with David Cooper he wrote *Reason and Violence*; in the Kingsley Hall project Esterson, Joseph Berke and Morton Schatzman were involved. Most of these collaborations were short-lived and each of the others mentioned developed their own independent careers but they were all associated with what came to be known as the movement of 'anti-psychiatry'.

The term 'anti-psychiatry' was coined by David Cooper. Under this banner many different practitioners and theoreticians from different countries grouped. The anti-psychiatrists held various, sometimes conflicting views but one particular line of reasoning is attributable to all of them – they all pitched their arguments against the power of the psychiatric establishment. They argued that the psychiatric diagnosis is scientifically meaningless. It is a way of labelling undesirable behaviour, under the guise of medical intervention. Those who are diagnosed ill are subjected to treatment which is a violation of human rights and dignity. The situation amounts to psychiatry having a mandate to declare some citizens unfit to live in an 'ordinary' community. It claims to cure but the supposed beneficiaries of that cure are often held in hospitals against their will. Within a structure like this it is impossible to understand the real nature of mental suffering and it is just as impossible to develop a coherent system of help.

From within the anti-psychiatric group various responses came, and they developed along two different, but related, lines. First, the anti-psychiatrists set out to re-evaluate our understanding of madness. Their views differed but they all developed ideas completely opposed to traditional psychiatry. Second, they attempted to establish forms of help (therapeutic communities, experimental wards, etc.), for those who are in mental distress, without recourse to the figure of the Doctor, and without the Hospital. These two are the emblematic figures around which the anti-psychiatric debate revolved.

The anti-psychiatric debate attracted enormous public attention. Laing was perceived as the spiritual leader of the movement and to an extent Laing's work is almost synonymous with anti-psychiatry. It is within this context that Laing will be presented here.

The term 'anti-psychiatry' has been criticized and rejected by almost all, including those that the term was meant to denote, Laing notwithstanding. According to one argument the psychiatrists working in hospitals are the actual anti-psychiatrists, as their function has nothing to do with healing. It has also been pointed out that the term 'anti-psychiatry' makes just as little sense as 'anti-science' or 'anti-medicine' to describe those that approach science or medicine differently. But although rejected, the term stuck. 'Anti-psychiatry' became very much part of the then current vocabulary. I shall also continue using it for three reasons. First, because of its wide usage at the time we find frequent references to it in literature; second, because no other term seems to quite fit ('radical psychiatry' or 'alternative psychiatry', for example, do not overlap with 'anti-psychiatry'); third, because in one respect the term is accurate: it highlights the 'anti-' aspect of these thinkers. They were all against establishment psychiatry or against establishment *tout court*.

III

Looking back at Laing's career it is obvious that his sabbatical year after Kingsley Hall was a turning point. In the time that followed Laing ceased to be engaged in any meaningful way in the field of psychiatry. He was no longer directly involved in therapeutic communities and his publications of the post-Ceylon period are in comparison to his earlier work trivial and do not add anything to his earlier career.

Furthermore, in some interviews he seemed to be backtracking from his previous position, or at least taking off the radical edge which was so characteristic of his approach. No, he did not share the views of the more politically minded psychiatrists, he did not belong to the left. Now he described his position as that of a sceptic. It was difficult to make out what actual views Laing did hold.

In a sense Laing's last book, the memoir *Wisdom, Madness and Folly*, is a relief. To an extent it was a return to form. Laing was not saying anything particularly new but the clarity of his writing was at its best and, more importantly, it dispels any feeling that Laing 'betrayed' the cause. In the first chapter he states his views:

> I never idealized mental suffering, or romanticised despair, dissolution, torture or terror. I have never said that parents or families or society 'cause' mental illness, genetically or environ-mentally. I have never denied the existence of patterns of mind and conduct that are excruciating. I have never called myself an anti-psychiatrist, and have disclaimed the term when my friend and colleague, David Cooper, introduced it. However, I agree with the anti-psychiatric thesis that by and large psychiatry functions to exclude and repress those elements society wants excluded and repressed. If society requires such exclusion then exclusion it will get, with or without the aid of psychiatry. Many psychiatrists want psychiatry to bow out of this function . . . Such a complete change of policy requires as complete a change of outlook, and that is rare.
>
> (WMF:8–9)

Although Laing was no longer active in the field, these views were consistent with his early work.

Why someone who was the exemplary figure of dissent and radical thinking should so suddenly cease to be active is an enigma. The difference between the earlier work of Laing and his career that followed after his return from India is such that it is hard to believe it comes from the same person. It is not that Laing radically changed his views, that he moved from the left to the right, for example. After returning from his sabbatical Laing never engaged in anything with the same intensity. It is that the brilliant light, so characteristic of his first offerings, simply went out. This is how it feels. Perhaps while in India Laing had some experiences which contributed to this; perhaps it was a case of burn-out. On reviewing his work one is impressed by how much Laing managed to do in so little time. In just over a decade he had published eight books and had set up and been involved for five years in the Kingsley Hall therapeutic community. Then comes the list of the less publicized activities and the immense work that was done behind the scenes. He went through full psychoanalytical training; he took part in recording, transcribing and then analysing hundreds of hours of interviews with families; he carried out a research programme into interpersonal perception; he conducted a study on family therapy. For three years he was the director of the psychotherapy centre, the Langham Clinic. Perhaps the work of these ten years was all that Laing had in him, perhaps at the age of forty-five he had said all.

Those who knew Laing will attest to an unusual personality. It was a mixture of undeniable charisma, brilliance and quite a savage streak. His intellect, his personality, made a great impression on others. He always drank more than was good for him and as the years went on this habit began to take its toll. This became more marked after his return from India. Laing's public appearances became quite often erratic or even disgraceful. There were occasions when he would appear drunk and abusive. To those who still cared for his views from the earlier days and hoped that the work would continue, this was a painful sight. One wonders if it was something to do with the pressure that his reputation exerted on him; whichever, the fire was not there any more. Whether that is what he experienced we cannot know, but there seemed to be some desperation in his inebriated public appearances, as though he was destroying, one could even say suiciding, his own image. One can speculate endlessly but finally this is not our concern. For those who are interested in the savage, murky side of Laing, there is a biography written by his son, Adrian (Laing 1994). There the reader will find an ample supply of stories about Laing's complicated personal life, about his financial difficulties, about his drunken stunts, but, except for two or three interesting professional anecdotes, not much else. The reader may prefer Laing's autobiography *Wisdom, Madness and Folly* and a recently published book of interviews with him which cover his personal as well as his professional career (Mullan 1995). One way or another, there is enough easily available material to speculate about Laing's personality. There is no need to include it in this book.[2]

IV

The Laing that we shall be exploring here is Laing the anti-psychiatrist. Presenting Laing within this context means that some of his activities will not be considered. In addition to being a psychiatrist Laing was one of the principal figures of the counter-culture of the 1960s; he was interested in Eastern philosophies; he was at one time interested in birth trauma; he ran breathing workshops, re-birthing workshops; his book *The Voice of Experience* belongs in a territory normally associated with what has become known as the New Age. These activities will not concern us. Furthermore, since nothing of real consequence, at least in the field of anti-psychiatry, came from Laing after his travel to the East, the presentation of his work will break off at the end of Kingsley Hall.

Some may say that to present not much more than a decade of Laing's work cannot be a comprehensive portrait. It may even be argued that this is a prejudiced choice. And so it is. It is based on the conviction that our interest in Laing today rests in his career as an anti-psychiatrist. And, at any rate, although it is a short period there are still a great many important issues that need to be analysed.

Various influences converged in Laing's work. In the earlier days he was very impressed with the European existentialist tradition; then he found great affinity with the family interactions research that was conducted in America; finally, he was familiar with the various critiques of the modern society in general and psychiatric practice in particular, which again were coming mostly from America. Laing was one of the key figures in the debate and it is relatively easy to reconstruct the intellectual climate in which he was doing his work, as well as the influences on his thinking, because he extensively referred to them himself.

It is less obvious how to frame his experiment at Kingsley Hall. The belief that people who normally end up in psychiatric hospitals could be helped outside the hospital setting was in that period becoming widespread. There was a sense of optimism, and various alternative projects were mushrooming everywhere, in Britain as well as abroad. In this case it is not the question of influence because most of these projects started after Kingsley Hall and many of them developed very differently. In choosing to present other alternative experiments I have opted for two which are as different from Laing's project as one can imagine. The first centres on the events around the Socialist Patients' Collective which was set up in Germany. The second is the Italian attempt to radically re-define and re-structure the whole psychiatric system. I have chosen them because they highlight the aspects of anti-psychiatry which Laing's work did not, namely, the political and social dimensions. These were certainly not Laing's strength.

To an extent this will amount to a presentation of the anti-psychiatric movement although the picture will not be full. One obvious omission is French anti-psychiatry. It is not included here because its distinct features (mainly the place of Lacanian psychoanalysis in it) would require extensive treatment which cannot be undertaken here. The reader interested in the subject can consult Sherry Turkle's *Psychoanalytic Politics. Freud's French Revolution* (Turkle 1979).

By way of rounding off I shall examine some of the responses to Laing as they came through various commentaries. The reactions to Laing were part of the 'Laing phenomenon'. In fact, he generated a kind of response that would merit a study in itself.

Since the heyday of anti-psychiatry the political and ideological climate has changed radically and today Laing may seem like some ancient dinosaur, typical of the 1960s' inconsequential noise that lacked substance. But it may well be the other way round, that is, the relative silence around Laing is more of a reflection of the times today than of the value of his work. Maybe it is time to re-visit some of those past figures that we have so happily buried (alive, since we are talking about ideas). This book is an attempt to show that his work merits to be re-viewed, re-examined and re-evaluated.

NOTES

1 The major sources for biographical information are Laing's own autobiography *Wisdom, Madness and Folly* and *Mad to be Normal* (Mullan 1995), a series of conversations with Laing tape-recorded during the last two years of his life.

2 [Added at proof stage.] A new biography, *R.D. Laing. A Divided Self* (London: Hodder & Stoughton, 1996) by John Clay has just appeared.

Chapter 2

The world of a psychotic

Schizophrenia

I

Any presentation of the work of Laing has to begin with some remarks, however preliminary, about psychiatry. Almost all of Laing's meaningful work is related to it.

Psychiatry, as we know it today, came into being at the beginning of the nineteenth century. The birth of the modern image of psychiatry is mostly associated with two names and two places – Philippe Pinel at Bicêstre in France and Samuel Tuke at the York Retreat. Before their time madmen and madwomen were viewed as deranged beasts beyond any help and the only solution was to have them locked up in dungeons or chained to a wall. Pinel and Tuke abolished physical constraints (chains, locked cells, etc.) and began to 'treat' the insane. With this development the image of the madperson changed considerably. He/she changed from a wild beast to a person who was sick and in need of help. Psychiatry's most important theoretical landmarks came a century later. In 1886 Emil Kraepelin published *Psychiatrie* (English translation *Lectures on Clinical Psychiatry* (Kraepelin 1905)) in which he proposed a classification of mental illnesses and identified the syndrome which he named 'dementia praecox'. In 1911 the Swiss psychiatrist Eugen Bleuler replaced the term 'dementia praecox' with 'schizophrenia' (Bleuler 1950). For all the criticism that Kraepelin's nosology has met and for all the revisions it has undergone, it has remained to this day the blueprint for psychiatry's taxonomical endeavours.

As far as treatment went it did not follow the example set by Pinel and Tuke, as a mixture of constraints (locked wards, padded cells, straitjackets) remained a norm. This was usually combined with physical handling (cold showers, wrapping up in wet blankets, etc.), possibly some form of organized activities to keep the patients busy,

such as work 'therapy', and rarer still, but sometimes attempted, some
forms of persuasion and moral improvement. The effects of these
treatments were at best negligible, the hospitals were overcrowded and
in general the conditions in these places were awful. The 1930s saw the
invention of interventions which affected the patient's physiology
directly – insulin-induced comas, lobotomy and electroshocks.[1] At the
beginning of the 1950s tranquillizing drugs were introduced. This
effected an enormous change. It quite quickly transpired that the new
drugs were no cure, but now psychiatrists did not have to resort to
heavy intervention and could instead help patients control their illness
through well-considered dosages of the new drugs.

The 'official' account of psychiatry's history would thus first tell us
about the enlightened views of Pinel and Tuke, of the methodological
achievements of Kraepelin and Bleuler, of the first crude attempts at direct
intervention through electroshocks and lobotomy, and the final breakthrough that came with the tranquillizers. Or something along these lines.

There is, however, a group of theoreticians, mostly historians, who
form a 'revisionist' trend in the historiography of psychiatry.[2] They
subject psychiatry to an altogether different type of scrutiny. These
studies tell us that the concept of mental illness developed according to
a logic that has nothing to do with science, but is an outcome of social
and economic changes in the society. In other words, mental illness is a
construct, not an 'objective' fact. They also raise the question of the
legal rights of patients who are detained without proper procedures and
whose consent is not sought when they are given treatment; they point
out the contradiction between healing and detention; they see in
psychiatry an oppressive force.

Different commentators focus on different themes, but in one respect
they are all in agreement – the most decisive moment in the history of
psychiatry was when the State handed over to the medical profession
the mandate to identify and treat madness. It happened in the nineteenth
century. In Britain, for example, the General Medical Bill, which gave
the medical profession the mandate to define and treat mental illness,
was passed in 1858. The medicalization of the profession did not
happen without opposition, there was no consensus, and many
expressed grave misgivings about medicine's competence to treat this
matter.[3] The Bill of 1858 succeeded after sixteen failed drafts and a
great deal of bitter dispute. Over a century has passed and psychiatry's
place in medicine is now a *fait accompli* but the doubts as to whether
this is really its rightful place remain. Too many, who would in other
circumstances fall into the clutches of psychiatry, get over their

difficulties without psychiatric intervention, either of their own devices, or on the psychoanalyst's couch, or some other form of non-medical therapy. Those who question the status of psychiatry argue that it is a pseudo-science operating with badly defined concepts and that its history is a history of incarceration, of oppression, and of crude intervention which often results in brain damage. Today most of psychiatry's more savage practices have been curtailed but this has not solved the questions. Psychiatry is more than just a branch of medicine. It is a vast edifice with an ideology, an attitude and, most of all, it is a language which shapes the reality it claims to describe.

II

Laing cut his teeth at the grim end of the profession. First medical training, next a period in neurology, then two years in a British Army psychiatric unit followed by two years in a regular hard-core psychiatric hospital. This was from 1952 to 1958, a period when the currently used tranquillizers were only just coming in. During this time Laing learnt to carry out neurological examinations, assisted in brain surgery, worked in an insulin unit, administered more or less all the pre-tranquillizer treatment then available – 'barbiturates, chloralhydrate, paraldehyde, electric shocks, "modified" insulin, straitjackets, "padded cells", injections, tube-feeds, amytal abreactions, antibuse, hypnosis' (WMF:94). He learnt to do all this and he began to doubt. Was it not a mistake to lump together neurology and psychiatry? In other words, was psychiatry, that is the care of the mentally ill, properly in the domain of medicine?

Laing described his professionally formative years in the autobio-graphical *Wisdom, Madness and Folly*, the last book he wrote before his death. He tells us about his aspirations, his fascination with literature and philosophy, his attempt to study under Karl Jaspers, and how he landed as a medic in a British Army Psychiatric Unit. Laing concludes the description of his stint in the army hospital with the following:

> The neck of the woods in which I had ended up for a mere two years was a place of misery, absurdity and humiliation. In my room in the officer's quarters, in the middle of the night, I would picture the other places, those barracks, those prisons, those other lunatic wards, those extermination wards, all those places of groans and tears that each night covers.

(WMF:110)

These were very difficult years. Later appointments – in the mental hospital and then in the Psychiatry Unit of Glasgow University – did not quite repeat the grimness of the earlier experience but by the time Laing left Glasgow for London he had seen all of the rough edge of the profession. At the end of his autobiography he tells us that by the time he was leaving Scotland he had already completed writing his first book, *The Divided Self*. However, if we were to read the books in reverse order, that is, first his autobiography and then *The Divided Self*, we would be hard put to find a continuity between them. Very little of the sentiments of the wretchedness of the psychiatric system comes through in *The Divided Self*. *The Divided Self* is a psychiatric text which aims to bring closer to the reader the world as experienced by a psychotic, with little reference to the absurdities of the psychiatric system that Laing saw. Part of the difference can be explained by the fact that the memoir was written some thirty years after the events. There is no reason to doubt the facts of Laing's account but they are seen through the prism of those thirty years. At the time, whatever misgivings he may have had, Laing was still well inside the psychiatric profession. *The Divided Self* is a measured study coming from a committed psychiatrist and for that reason it belongs in psychiatric literature.

But although the book's form is classical – it is basically a monograph on a psychiatric condition – it is driven by a radical streak. Coming from within the profession, Laing undertook to interrogate the founding structure of psychiatry's discourse – its language. To analyse the language of psychiatry means to subject to scrutiny its very reality. The title of the opening chapter of *The Divided Self* 'The existential-phenomenological foundations for a science of persons' makes Laing's intentions quite clear: psychiatry must be based on a 'science of persons', and, as the contents of the chapter go to show, Laing is of the view that the foundations of this science are in language. So while neurology, considered to be psychiatry's close cousin, has a basis in natural science, psychiatry is formed almost entirely from the way we speak about madness. The language of psychopathology which Laing learnt to use in his medical training is a depersonalized language.

How can one demonstrate the general human relevance and significance of the patient's condition if the words one has to use are specifically designed to isolate and circumscribe the meaning of the patient's life to a particular clinical entity?

(DS:18)

These clinical entities may sound as rigorous and clear as any other medical terminology but in fact they are nothing of the sort. We name some individuals 'schizophrenic' or 'psychotic' but these are no more than vague terms which not only tell us nothing about the predicament of those they are meant to describe but estrange us from them even more. Those who are subjected to this language experience it as degradation and humiliation. Laing supplies an example from one of the key texts of modern psychiatry, Kraepelin's *Lectures on Clinical Psychiatry* (1905). There Kraepelin gives a description of an interview he is having with a hospital inmate. The interview takes place in front of a group of medical students. The patient is asked the simplest of questions, whether he knows where he is, what his name is. Instead of intelligible answers Kraepelin gets in return a diatribe which he takes to be a 'series of disconnected sentences having no relation whatever to the general situation' (DS:30). Laing proceeds to demonstrate that with a little imagination we can see that the patient's reaction is a perfectly coherent response. He is treated as an exhibit for the edification of the students, he is asked trivial questions. His outburst is an ironic reaction to the situation he finds himself in; it most certainly is not a 'sign' or 'symptom' of some disease. What Laing concludes from this example is best summed up in the following passage:

> The standard texts contain the descriptions of the behaviour of people in a behavioural field that includes the psychiatrist. The behaviour of the patient is to some extent a function of the behaviour of the psychiatrist in the same behavioural field. The standard psychiatric patient is a function of a standard psychiatrist, and of the standard mental hospital. The figured base, as it were, which underscores all Bleuler's great description of schizophrenics is his remark that when all is said and done they were stranger to him than the birds in his garden.
>
> (DS:28)

Within two pages Laing mentions in the context of his argument Kraepelin and Bleuler, the two towering figures of modern psychiatry. This cannot be a coincidence; the lasting influence of these two remains embedded in the language psychiatry uses today. It is interesting to note that Laing does not criticize any particular concept that comes from Kraepelin and Bleuler. Instead he homes in on the one issue that is at the core of his argument: whatever scientific value there might be in psychiatry's findings, they suffer from a fundamental flaw – they study the patient outside the context of his life in general, and outside the context of the psychiatrist–patient relationship in particular. Every psychiatric description, Laing will go on to argue, is not a statement of fact but an interpretation, and the interpretations we find in the psychiatric textbooks are determined in advance by the categories of the theoretical stance and by the language.

> It is just possible to have a thorough knowledge of what has been discovered about the hereditary or familial incidence of manic-depressive psychosis or schizophrenia, to have a facility in recognizing schizoid 'ego distortion' and schizophrenic ego defects, plus the various 'disorders' of thought, memory, perceptions, etc., to know, in fact, just about everything that can be known about the psychopathology of schizophrenia or of schizophrenia as a disease without being able to understand one single schizophrenic.
>
> (DS:33)

To understand a schizophrenic it is necessary, first of all, to realize that no-one *has* schizophrenia, one *is* schizophrenic. Schizophrenia is a way of being, a way of experiencing the world. This experience can be rendered comprehensible but for this we have to find a new language and reject the terminology which we have inherited from the traditional school.

III

Before Laing begins the exploration of this 'is-ness' of schizophrenia he concentrates on how we come to recognize a psychotic. This happens when there is a breakdown of communication between two persons. The cases in psychiatry textbooks are cases of a breakdown of communication between the patient and the psychiatrist. The breakdown occurs along very specific lines – it is when there is no mutual recognition of each other's identity. When two sane people meet, argues Laing, this recognition takes place. It is not necessarily exact, but it is good enough. Laing gives some examples of the kind of lack of recognition that leads to charges of insanity.

> he says he is Napoleon, whereas I say he is not;
> *or if* he says I am Napoleon, whereas I say I am not;
> *or if* he thinks that I wish to seduce him, whereas I think I have given him no grounds in actuality for supposing that such is my intention;
> *or if* he thinks that I am afraid he will murder me, whereas I am not afraid of this, and have given him no reason to think that I am.

And then Laing adds:

> I suggest, therefore, that *sanity or psychosis is tested by the degree of conjunction or disjunction between two persons where the one is sane by common consent.*
>
> (DS:36, italics in the original)

This is the kind of statement that can take us in many directions. We may wonder what this common consent which attests to sanity is worth; we may also wonder how this degree of conjunction or disjunction occurs. At this point of his deliberations Laing leaves such questions unanswered and instead focuses on the nature of this disjunction. The fact that one of the two protagonists is sane and the other is not is a premise that Laing accepts.

So, although we find in *The Divided Self* a clearly articulated opposition to the traditional psychiatric terminology, the book is written with an explicit acceptance of the validity of the term 'schizophrenia'. It means something to Laing, it refers to a particular fashion of being-in-the-world, and it is a state quite different from sanity. Schizophrenia is a valid term and therefore it is possible to speak about it in terms which are general, without, however, losing sight of what it means to experience this form of being-in-the-world. *The Divided Self* is not intended as a monograph on all that comes under the rubric of 'schizophrenia' in psychiatric textbooks. It concentrates on the conditions which lead to the onset of this particular experience and in this respect the boundaries of the enquiry are clearly outlined. Laing states in the Preface:

> The present book is a study of schizoid and schizophrenic persons; its basic purpose is to make madness, and the process of going mad, comprehensible . . . No attempt is made to present a comprehensive theory of schizophrenia. No attempt is made to explore constitutional and organic aspects.
>
> (DS:9)

Laing accepts the term schizophrenia and likewise he takes sanity to be a valid term; before undertaking an analysis of a schizophrenic experience he sets out to roughly define what a sane person is like. His notion of sanity is not derived from pathology (lack of illness), or sociology (the norm, role functioning), or psychoanalysis (ego boundaries, defences); instead it is couched in quite simple existential terms. A sane person will:

experience his being as real, alive, whole; as differentiated from the rest of the world in ordinary circumstances so clearly that his identity and autonomy are never in question; as a continuum in time; as having an inner consistency, substantiality, genuineness, and worth; as spatially co-extensive with the body; and, usually, as having begun in or around birth and liable to extinction with death.

(DS:41–42)

Laing calls this state 'ontological security'. What determines it cannot quite be said exactly but it is clear that it is acquired early in life, in childhood, and it is what constitutes an existential base. A person who is ontologically secure will be able to face most adversaries of life without the loss of a sense of reality, of his own or of others, and of the world in general. Extreme situations may provoke this loss but usually only temporarily. There are, however, those who do not feel alive, whole and consistent; who do not experience themselves as embodied and separate from others. In such instances we should speak of the state of 'ontological insecurity'. It takes on different forms and it is the root of the kind of behaviour which comes to be judged to be mad. Laing sets out to explore different modes of ontological insecurity.

This marks a change of direction of the book. In the opening arguments Laing conceived of psychosis as a breakdown in communication, as something that happens between people. Now the focus shifts to the 'inner' world of the psychotic and at this point *The Divided Self* turns into a clinical study. In this respect it is not very different from other studies, as it is structured along orthodox lines – it is a theoretical treatise supported with abundant case illustrations.

IV

To live in a state of ontological insecurity, or to have a low threshold of security, means to experience perpetual threat. This threat comes either from other persons, or from the external world as a whole. A person who is ontologically insecure may avoid all contact with others for fear of being engulfed by them. So any form of closeness is experienced as a risk to one's identity, a relation of intimacy turns into a fight for survival, personal relations cannot bring any sense of gratification. Another form of experiencing this sense of ontological insecurity is when one's identity is felt to be a complete vacuum. Experienced from this position reality persecutes, it is implosive, threatening to fill in and obliterate, as it were, whatever sense of identity there may be. Finally, such a person may feel dead, turned to stone, or a robot. Relations with others objectify one's existence further, turning one into a mere unfeeling cog in the wheel, a dead thing without any sense of autonomy. Since such a person is not capable of authentic responses, the way to avoid them is to have others turned to stone so they will not impinge. Laing grouped these forms of anxiety under three headings: 'engulfment', 'implosion', 'petrification and depersonalization' (DS:43–49).

To live and cope constantly with the sense of ontological insecurity necessitates some very particular strategies. It is impossible to altogether avoid contact with reality and with others; ways have to be found where some semblance of contact can be maintained without putting the fragile identity at risk. This is achieved through the process of splitting, described in psychiatry as schizoid splitting. It is as though a schizoid person is trying to drive a bargain. He designates part of himself to the external world but himself dissociates from this part; in a sense there is an entity which to all intents and purposes could be thought of as an 'I' but which is disowned as not belonging to the 'real I'.

This breaking into separate parts happens around two basic splits that are characteristic of a schizoid personality. The first is the split between the body and the mind. This can develop to such an extent that the body is felt as an alien being, belonging to the outside world which is experienced as just as alien. Laing describes this as the 'unembodied self'. Again, as in the case of 'ontological insecurity', Laing first tells us what it is like to be an embodied person, in the ordinary sense:

> The embodied person has a sense of being flesh and blood and bones, of being biologically alive and real: he knows himself to be substantial. To the extent that he is thoroughly 'in' his body, he is likely to have a sense of personal continuity in time. He will experience himself as subject to the dangers that threaten his body, the dangers of attack, mutilation, disease, decay and death. He is implicated in bodily desire, and the gratifications and frustrations of the body. The individual thus has as his starting-point an experience of his body as a base from which he can be a person with other human beings.
>
> (DS:67)

It is enough to state some or all of this in the negative and the picture of an unembodied self is clear. The person who is dissociated from the body may be completely indifferent to pain or disease; sexuality may be renounced, or practised, as 'mechanical', without the slightest feeling of pleasure coming into it. Such a person will also become hyper-conscious. The body is now 'out-there' in the world, to be seen, caught in a double gaze, the gaze of the self which can now only perceive the body as foreign, and the gaze of the others.

The other split concerns the experience of the self. As the self feels constantly threatened it splits into two. It keeps a 'true self' and develops a separate 'false self system' which will act like a façade behind which the 'true self' can hide. This may manifest itself in various ways. It may be an excessive propensity to act according to what one thinks others expect one to do. Such a person will take on and live out assumed roles, perhaps impersonate others. While these strategies to deal with others are developed the 'real self' becomes increasingly buried. It is protected and felt to be free but, deprived of any contact with the real world, it shrivels up and all that it has left in the end is a feeling of guilt which is a response to the inauthenticity of its existence.

These splits can sometimes allow for some sort of functioning in the world. However, it is more likely that, once they set in, they will continue to develop. The schism between the real and the false self grows deeper. The schizoid organization of a personality turns into a psychosis. The separate bits start acting independently of each other. Speech can become affected and mannered, as though foreign, and may even break down altogether into a 'word-salad'. Or conversely such a person may completely withdraw, seemingly losing all interest in his or her surroundings. Psychosis is thus a particular way of being where all the interactions take the form of splits – splits between the real and the false self, between the real self and the body which becomes part of the false self, between the false self and others. And the true self, the remnants of which are somehow always there, experiences despair, anguish, guilt, terror and profound insecurity. It wants to be alive but it cannot find the means to be so.

V

Laing's descriptions are heavily indebted to the existential and phenomenological tradition. He draws his inspiration from the philosophers Sartre, Heidegger, Merleau-Ponty and Kierkegaard; the theologian Tillich; the psychiatrists Binswanger and Minkowski.[4] He found in their writings a sensibility in describing the human existence which renders them appropriate for the exploration of the world of the psychotic. He does not cite them often but many of his theoretical discussions are heavily indebted to them. Laing does not appear to adhere strictly to the thinking of any particular philosopher. It is more that he takes from one or another some issue in relation to the clinical material that he is considering. The distinction between the authentic and inauthentic comes from Heidegger. The chapter on self-consciousness is Laing's attempt to discuss the problem around the nature of the gaze, of how a look can affirm or turn into stone, of the wish to be invisible as well as the fear of it (DS:106–119); the treatment of the problem owes a great deal to Sartre. The concept of the embodied and unembodied self seems to come largely from the analyses of Merleau-Ponty. The concept of 'ontological security' comes from Tillich. Many of the descriptions of the patients show Laing's feel for Kierkegaard, as well as his sensitivity for the patients.

Laing's allegiance to the existential tradition is also very marked in his conception of guilt. He does not present a clear account of his own position, but the question comes up in several places and the gist of his views is the following.

One can distinguish between 'authentic' and 'inauthentic' guilt. The 'inauthentic' or 'false' guilt is generated by the false self system. The sense of guilt that psychoanalysis speaks about is presumably a 'false' guilt, although Laing does not say so in so many words. He states, however, that 'one will have to be careful to avoid regarding the inner self as the source of "genuine" or true guilt' (DS:93). In another place we find a comment which makes a little clearer what Laing has in mind. After a case discussion ('The case of Peter', DS:120–133), which describes a young psychotic man entangled in countless false self systems, Laing concludes with the following remark:

> Guilt is the call of Being for itself in silence, says Heidegger. What one might call Peter's *authentic guilt* was that he had capitulated to his *inauthentic guilt*, and was making it the aim of his life not to be himself.

(DS:132)

So it seems that Laing conceives genuine guilt as a consequence of the abandonment of one's authenticity. It is not a psychological phenomenon in the sense of being permanently seated in some psychological structure, say, the super-ego. It arises in relation to how one lives out one's potentiality.

It would be easy to conclude from this brief survey of the influences of existential thought on Laing that he was eclectic and superficial. But it is not quite like that. We could show that Sartre had a particularly big influence on his work, yet he is not attempting to be a Sartrean psychiatrist; he develops after Heidegger a penchant for hyphenated terms (being-for-itself, being-for-other, etc.)[5] but he is not trying to be a Heideggerian psychiatrist either. Laing borrowed from diverse sources to develop his own language. This language is very persuasive and there is great merit in his ability to bring together the often obscure existential terminology and the concrete case descriptions. In effect he is far less philosophically precious than some of the existential psychiatrists from the Continent.

VI

Laing's relation to existential philosophy is quite simple – he agrees with its basic tenets and then freely borrows from it for his purposes, which are not philosophical but clinical. His relation to psychoanalysis, however, is a little more complex.

After coming from Glasgow Laing entered psychoanalytical training with the Institute of Psycho-Analysis. He went through his own analysis (with Charles Rycroft) and had his work supervised by two senior colleagues (Marion Milner and D.W. Winnicott). He was also employed at the Tavistock Institute which was always a psychoanalytically oriented clinic. For a period of a few years Laing rubbed shoulders with the cream of the psychoanalytical establishment.[6] But although he went through and completed the training, at no point in his career did he fully espouse the doctrine and always expressed deep reservations about it. Here, for instance, is a comment which in some respects is characteristic of one attitude to psychoanalysis that Laing adopts. After presenting the facts of a case of a woman patient, he opens the discussion with the following remarks:

> An intensive application of what is often supposed to be the classical psycho-analytic theory of hysteria to this patient might attempt to show this woman as unconsciously libidinally bound to her father; with, consequently, unconscious guilt and unconscious need and/ or fear of punishment. Her failure to develop lasting libidinal relationships away from her father would seem to support this first view, along with her decision to live with him, to take her mother's place, as it were, and the fact that she spent most of her day, as a woman of twenty-eight, actually thinking about him. Her devotion to her mother in her last illness would be partly the consequences of

unconscious guilt at her unconscious ambivalence to her mother; and her anxiety at her mother's death would be anxiety at her unconscious wish for her mother's death coming true. And so on.

(DS:56)

This is obviously a caricature of psychoanalytical thinking and to this Laing adds what seems a mocking footnote where he refers the reader to an article by a leading exponent of Kleinian theory, Hanna Segal, 'for extremely valuable psycho-analytic contributions to apparently "hysterical" symptom formation'.

Such jibes at psychoanalysis are not frequent in *The Divided Self* but from the few that there are some issues are clear. Laing is of the view that the language of psychoanalysis is just as guilty of alienating the patients as is the language of psychiatry. Talk of a separate realm of the 'unconscious' only introduces another split. As far as the patient discussed above is concerned, Laing will say:

the central or pivotal issue in this patient's life is not to be discovered in her 'unconscious'; it is lying quite open for her to see, as well as for us (although this is not to say that there are not many things about herself that this patient does not realize).

(DS:56)

Laing rejects the metapsychology of psychoanalysis. His commitment to existentialism does not allow him to accept it. The way he addresses the question of guilt makes this quite clear. What lies at the heart of a psychotic experience has nothing to do with unconscious guilt or some other unconscious factor but comes from the primary lack of ontological security. The subsequent development of false selves in order to deal with the insecurity puts the psychotic in an inauthentic life and it is this which generates guilt. In this sense guilt is in a way simultaneous with psychotic developments. In other words, it is an existential, not a psychological, predicament. The shift from psychoanalysis to existentialism is also a shift from the 'inner' in the psychological sense to the space of interaction of the psychotic with his/her world.

Another line of disagreement with psychoanalysis follows from the influence of Harry Stack Sullivan on Laing's ideas. Sullivan, active in the 1930s and 1940s, was one of the key figures in American psychiatry and his influence has been considerable. His relation to psychoanalysis (and to Kraepelin) was similar to the stance Laing came to adopt. When Sullivan appeared on the scene American psychiatry was held in a stranglehold created by the teachings of Kraepelin and Freud. Both held schizophrenia as incurable, either because it was a degenerative organic disease (Kraepelin) or because schizophrenics were unable to form transference (Freud). Sullivan's critique of Kraepelin focused on Kraepelin's inability to see the life context of the patient; he reproached Freud for privileging the 'inner' reality over the interpersonal space. Sullivan broke this state of affairs through systematically developing a theoretical body of work and new psychotherapeutic approaches to psychotic patients.

However, much as Laing criticizes psychoanalysis, in some respects he follows its insights. For example, the distinction between the true and false self system is in its outline the same as we find in the writings of Winnicott. Laing's views on psychotic developments largely converge with the views of the other analysts who worked with psychotic patients – Frieda Fromm-Reichmann, Harry Stack Sullivan, Paul Federn, John Rosen. He also refers frequently to the theories of the analysts from the Middle Group.[7] But most of all Laing is in agreement with psychoanalysis's basic contention that sanity and insanity begin in childhood within the context of the family. He does not follow the Freudian route of the unresolved Oedipal conflict (or, more precisely in the case of psychosis, the notion of a pre-Oedipal disturbance) or Melanie Klein's pre-given paranoid-schizoid position; Laing's thinking follows a similar line to Winnicott's idea of a facilitating environment, although apparently there was no direct influence.[8] It is similar in that Laing locates the source of an ontologically insecure being in the family's/mother's failure to give the child the first sense of security in the world. Laing also admits of the possibility of some biological inborn factors due to which babies differ in their capacity to demand gratification and which may make it difficult to gratify the child's needs. But it is the mother and the total family situation which may help or prevent the development of these capacities:

> there may be some ways of being a mother that impede rather than facilitate or 'reinforce' any genetically determined inborn tendency there may be in the child towards achieving the primary developmental stages of ontological security. Not only the mother but also the total family situation may impede rather than facilitate the child's capacity to participate in a real shared world, as self-with-other.

(DS:189)

n the family that the diagnosis of madness first takes
observed a certain pattern in the development of
e 'good-bad-mad' scenario. The 'good' period is when
ever makes demands, is quiet, never ever gives any trouble.
nes a 'bad' spell, an outbreak of violent behaviour. It most
akes the form of a tirade of accusations against the mother, the
father or both parents. From being good the child becomes wicked. This
is the point where the parents decide that something is wrong with the
child and consult a specialist, a psychiatrist. The diagnosis is made and
the child is now recognized as mad. When reformulated into the child's
way of experiencing the world, this simple scheme of things tells us the
following. At the beginning the child's demands were not recognized
and were consequently smothered. As a response the child begins to
develop a false self system set. This self system acquiesces and creates
the impression of a good child that never gives any problem. At a
certain point, usually quite suddenly, the true self makes an attempt to
free itself from the constraining false self and the equally constraining
influence of the parents who nourish this false self. The parents are
accused of being controlling, of being stifling, of not allowing the child
to live. This comes to the parents as a shock, as a sign of ingratitude.
How can such a good child come up with such unfair and preposterous
accusations? Incomprehensible. From there the point is quickly reached
where instead of being simply bad, there is something wrong with the
child. Then it takes only one more step. The psychiatrist is called in and
a psychiatric career begins.

VII

If we further analyse Laing's relation to psychoanalysis we will find that
in some respects his shift to existentialism does not so much move the
problematic into a different terrain but simply reverses values, in the
sense that Laing retains psychoanalysis's notion of a psychic interiority
but attributes to it different values. This is evident in his notion of the
'true self'.

The self, as long as it is 'uncommitted to the objective element', is
free to dream and imagine anything. Without reference to the
objective element it can be all things to itself – it has unconditioned
freedom, power, creativity. But its freedom and its omnipotence are
exercised in a vacuum and its creativity is only the capacity to
produce phantoms. The *inner honesty, freedom, omnipotence*, and

creativity, which the 'inner' self cherishes as its ideals, are cancelled, therefore, by a coexisting tortured sense of self-duplicity, of the lack of any real freedom, of utter impotence and sterility.

(DS:89, italics in the original)

Laing's notion of 'true self' is *mutatis mutandis* the same as the notion of the unconscious in that it is a conception of selfhood which is formed around some essential, immutable, but never directly observed or experienced inner core. Freud conceived of this essential being as a savage instinctual realm that needs restraining. According to Laing the self, the true self, is endowed with honesty, freedom, creativity. Laing's postulate of this true self may be appealing but its theoretical grounding is no sounder than the Freudian unconscious to which he objects. Furthermore, it may feed an illusion that there is a real self waiting to blossom as soon as the false self has been stripped away, whereas in reality there is probably no such thing. If a psychotic were to dismantle the patchwork of feigned personalities and borrowed languages that make up his world, then he would most likely find himself staring at a nothingness that has little to do with freedom and creativity.

In later years this problem reappears in Laing's thinking, although in quite a different form.

VIII

As with any work, one may level all sorts of criticism at *The Divided Self*, but this could not diminish the exceptional quality of Laing's exposition. This existential and phenomenological analysis of the world of the psychotic is a classic of psychiatric literature, and, in English at least, it has no equal. Written in a limpid style it brings its divergent intellectual influences – psychopathology, psychoanalysis and existialism, an analysis of the development of psychosis, a critique of the profession – into a seamless narrative. Of its type *The Divided Self* is probably the book most widely read, by professionals and laymen alike. One of the sources of the immense success it enjoys comes from its powerful plea for the understanding of the world as experienced by a psychotic. No commentary can convey the sensitivity and insight that is behind Laing's writing. A friend of mine, a psychologist who has had several nervous breakdowns, who has been hospitalized on numerous occasions and diagnosed with almost every conceivable mental illness, has said to me that of the many books that he has read only Laing spoke about him, all the others spoke about his illness. This is probably not an untypical response; many other hospital patients must have recognized themselves in the book. The cases that Laing presents are vivid and his empathy is evident.

The last chapter, 'The ghost of a weed garden: a study of a chronic schizophrenic', is the most impressive. It is an analysis of a twenty-six-year-old girl who had been in hospital for nine years with a diagnosis of schizophrenia. She had very little 'treatment', just a course of insulin, and thereafter she no more than just vegetated on the ward. She was withdrawn, inaccessible, she hallucinated. 'In clinical psychiatric terminology, she suffered from depersonalization; derealization; autism; nihilistic delusions; delusions of persecution, omnipotence; she had ideas of reference and end-of-the-world fantasies; auditory hallucinations; impoverishment of affects, etc.' (DS:178). Her being was so fragmented that Laing described it as 'living a death-in-life existence in a state approaching chaotic nonentity' (DS:195). Laing interviewed her family and it is in the course of analysing this case that he presented the 'good-bad-mad' pattern.

Above all one is struck by Laing's sensitivity to the patient. He offers a phenomenological analysis of a splintered being and through it he penetrates her seemingly incomprehensible speech, her schizophrenese. She would say things that seemed to make no sense and came across as a jumble of disconnected statements. She would refer to herself in the first, second or third person; claimed to be an 'occidental sun'; called herself 'Mrs Taylor'. In his lengthy analysis Laing shows how this incoherent speech was a reflection of a personality broken into separated, seemingly independent parts. Some of the utterances had quite precise meanings. For example, in the course of interviewing the family he discovered that Julie's mother described her pregnancy with Julie as 'wanted and not wanted', meaning that the pregnancy was accidental and that she wanted a son out of it. So Julie was an 'occidental sun'; she was 'Mrs Taylor' because she felt she was tailor-made by her mother. On the whole she presented a picture of complete psychological devastation and Laing tells us what he thinks was the principal reason for her ending in such a state:

> What I feel must have been the most schizophrenic factor of this time [during the 'bad' phase] was not simply Julie's attack on her mother, or even her mother's counter-attack, but the complete absence of anyone in her world who could or would see some sense in her point of view, whether it was right or wrong.

(DS:192)

It is interesting how in the sea of psychotic symptoms Laing manages to keep his eye on this simple factor. This also explains why he was able to establish a rapport with a patient in such a wretched state. To then move the reader with an account of this state is a testimony to a very unusual level of empathy.[9] Laing could really see something that others did not, and what he saw was quite straightforward, coming from a simple unprejudiced gaze.

NOTES

1 One wonders if it is a coincidence that psychiatry's two most barbaric inventions, electroshock treatment and lobotomy, were introduced in countries under a Fascist regime – the first was invented by Cerletti in Mussolini's Italy, the second by Egas Moniz in the Portugal of Salazar.

2 The list of authors who have dealt specifically with the developments of nineteenth-century psychiatry is quite long. Hunter and Macalpine (1963), Scull (1982), Skultans (1975) are the principal texts.

3 Select Committees were set up to examine the question of medical supervision of the care of the mentally ill. One lay member had this to say:

> I think they are most unfit of any class of persons. In the first place, from every enquiry I have made, I am satisfied that medicine has little or no effect on the disease, and the only reason for their selection is the confidence which is placed in their being able to apply a remedy to the malady. They are all persons interested more or less. It is extremely difficult in examining either the public Institutions or private houses not to have a strong impression on your mind, that medical men derive a profit in some shape or form from those different establishments . . . The rendering therefore, [of] any interested class of persons the Inspectors and Controllers, I hold to be mischievous in the greatest possible degree.
>
> (Treacher and Baruch 1981:127)

4 The titles most relevant are: *Being and Nothingness* (Sartre 1962), *Being and Time* (Heidegger 1962), *The Phenomenology of Perception* (Merleau-Ponty 1962), *The Sickness unto Death* (Kierkegaard 1954), *The Courage to Be* (Tillich 1952), *Being in the World* (Binswanger 1963), *Lived Time* (Minkowski 1970) and an important collection *Existence – A New Dimension in Psychiatry and Psychology* (May *et al.* 1958).

5 Laing expressed a dislike for hyphenated terms: 'we have an already shattered Humpty Dumpty who cannot be put together by any number of hyphenated or compound words: psycho-physical, psycho-somatic, psycho-biological, psycho-pathological, psycho-social, etc., etc.' (DS:20) but at times he uses somewhat similar language. And although its provenance is different, it is the point where he is least faithful to the plain English in which he intended to present his work and which is one of the attractive features of *The Divided Self*.

6 Laing gives an account of his time at the Tavistock Clinic and of his training in *Mad to be Normal* (Mullan 1995:143–161).

7 The Middle Group refers to an informal group of analysts who formed after a somewhat acrimonious split between Anna Freud and Melanie Klein. They did not take sides in the dispute and developed what became known as the 'object relations' approach. Harry Guntrip, Ronald Fairbairn, Marion Milner and Michael Balint were the most distinguished of the first generation. In some respects Winnicott could be considered the principal figure of this group.

8 The similarities between Laing's and Winnicott's ideas are clear, particularly the idea of a true and false self. But in a later interview Laing claimed that he had his basic position worked out before he had come to know Winnicott's writings. For example, the distinction between the true and false self, he explained, was more an attempt to translate the Heideggerian notions of authenticity and inauthenticity (Mullan 1995:152). Since Laing seemed quite open in terms of his influences there is no reason to doubt this claim.

9 Laing referred to this case many years later in an interview. The relationship with this particular patient was, in his own estimation, what 'gives that book the heart' (Mullan 1995:266).

Chapter 3

Knots

I

Laing began and virtually completed *The Divided Self* while he was employed in a psychiatric hospital in Glasgow. This one book constitutes an entire phase of Laing's work. His next appointment was at the Tavistock Clinic in London and it was an altogether different setting. The Tavistock was (and is) an exclusively out-patient organization and Laing ceased to have any contact with the type of patient he had encountered earlier in the psychiatric hospitals. In the new post his time was divided between clinical out-patient work and research.

The Divided Self is woven around the idea that the schizophrenic is a person whose inner potentiality has been destroyed and the book presents an analysis of this inner devastation. The research that Laing undertook at the Tavistock focused on something different – patterns of interpersonal communication and perception. The governing thought behind this new approach was that persons cannot be studied in isolation, outside their social context and most of all their family. This is particularly important when the study of persons with a psychiatric problem is undertaken, because if there is a disturbance it is a disturbance of the network of communications that this person is in. In other words, the so-called psychiatric 'illness' is not an internal affair but it is a way in which people perceive each other and interact with each other.

The subject of these investigations was already well signalled in *The Divided Self*. There Laing argued persuasively that the diagnosis of psychosis is as much the effect of the encounter between the psychiatrist and the patient as anything else. It was already clear to Laing that there is no sound justification for speaking of schizophrenia as a definable illness which the person 'carries'. A psychiatric illness is pronounced within a relation between two, or more, people. But Laing did not just develop ideas which were already present in *The Divided Self*, he significantly changed his perspective. In the first book he argued that 'sanity or psychosis is tested by the degree of conjunction or disjunction between two persons where the one is sane by common consent' (DS:36). This line of argument will be taken further, but with a difference. At the earlier stage Laing accepted that there was something like a psychosis, and so he saw the disjunction between two persons to be provoked by the psychotic's way of experiencing the world. However, psychiatry was methodologically ill-equipped to come to grips with the problem. In the next phase of his work Laing altogether suspended any notion of the psychotic experience, and consequently he abandoned any attempt to analyse the 'inner world' of the psychotic. He also moves away from existentialism. There will be no longer any talk of 'authentic guilt' or true self. In *Self and Others*, the work that appeared after *The Divided Self*, there are virtually no references to the existential and phenomenological tradition and the only significant comment that Laing offers makes the change quite apparent:

> The space, geometrical and metaphorical, of both adult and child, is highly structured by the influence of others, one way or another, all the time. This is 'common sense', a truism, but it becomes necessary to state this when a phenomenology of space neglects to give due weight to this factor.

And he adds to this a footnote:

> In particular I refer to the pioneering studies of Minkowski. The same criticism is applicable to Binswanger.

(SO:135)

This sums up Laing's change of heart quite well. The psychiatrists of the phenomenological school whose influence was so prominent in the early work are now criticized for neglecting the importance of the actions of others on our lives. And so, while in *The Divided Self* Laing argues that no-one *has* schizophrenia but rather that one *is* schizophrenic, in *Self and Others* he would no longer consider this valid because the *is-ness* of the person rests in the actual communication he or she is in. The concept of 'selfhood', so central to the first book, is dissolved in this network of communications. The word 'phenomenology' still comes up occasionally with the difference that at this stage of his project Laing will speak of a phenomenology of relations, or social phenomenology.

Self and Others was published only a year after *The Divided Self* and all these changes in direction are already fully spelt out. As though to underline his disagreement with the attempts to place the essence of the human's existence 'inside' the person, Laing begins with a chapter entitled 'Phantasy and experience' which is an engagement with psychoanalysis, more precisely with the notion of the 'unconscious phantasy' as developed within the Melanie Klein group. The actual text which Laing subjects to scrutiny is a paper by Susan Isaacs, 'The Nature and Function of Phantasy' (Isaacs 1952), considered a fair and succinct exposition of the theoretical position that this particular group of analysts took. That Laing would discuss their theoretical stance is not surprising because it was exactly this group that he had most to do with while he underwent his own psychoanalytic training.

The notion of unconscious phantasy was first developed by Freud and has become an important feature of the Kleinian version of psychoanalysis. Phantasies are the primary content of unconscious processes and exert a continuous influence on psychic activity. They fashion our relation to reality and they are at the core of mental disturbances. The one marked legacy of Isaacs' paper is that she introduced the particular spelling ('phantasy') which differentiates it from our ordinary understanding of a fantasy.[1] Laing takes up Isaacs' presentation chiefly because she regards unconscious phantasy as a mode of experience, an experience which is unconscious and which therefore is not known to the subject, although its existence can be inferred by some other person. The gist of Laing's disagreement with this scheme is that it is set up around a series of dualities. Closely sticking to Isaacs' text he shows that throughout her exposition there is a somewhat mysterious passage from the inner world to the outer, from the mental to the physical, from the ungraspable figment to an experience which can be handled, touched and seen. This passage is explained by a series of mechanisms such as conversion, introjection and projection, 'mechanisms' which Laing does not think explain anything and only obscure the problem still further. Of course, Laing knows perfectly well that people are at one time or another unaware of certain things but instead of resorting to the notion of the unconscious, he will go on to say that in a 'rough and ready way' people are split and, therefore, they are not always communicating with themselves very well. The splits are not permanent; at times people are not aware of things only to be able to recall them later. They can do so when the split is healed, 'once a split is dissolved in the present, memory is *always* present to some extent' (SO:32). But there are always some splits, 'the difficulty is that as some doors open, others close' (SO:32).

It is not easy to unravel exactly how Laing conceives of these phenomena because he is prone to quick and simple statements without much elaboration or development. For example, the idea that memory is linked to communicational processes, rather than being some inner reservoir of stored up images, is very interesting and certainly consistent with Laing's attempt to move out of the realm of 'selfhood'. But Laing only states it and moves on. He further places the question of memory in the sphere of the interpersonal:

> Some people seem to have a 'way with them', so that somehow or other in their presence others seem to be able to remember what they so often forget, and seem to know, while imagining, *that* they are imagining, and *what* they are imagining.

> (SO:31)

What this 'way with them' is Laing does not quite spell out but it is clear from the rest of what he says that these people have the knack of opening the lines of communications, so to speak, as to Laing 'the "unconscious" is what we do not communicate, to ourselves or to one another' (SO:32).

What can we communicate or infer? An experience, of which there are many different modes. Thinking, feeling, imagining, fantasizing, dreaming, remembering, perceiving are all different modes of experience. While I can experience myself directly this is not true of the experience of the other; I have no access to them and therefore I cannot experience his or her experience directly. The other can communicate an experience to me, I can infer someone's experience, or attribute it to the other. The arena of experience can be either private or public, though the boundary between the two is fluid and subject to many perturbations.

II

Unlike *The Divided Self*, *Self and Others* does not read easily. It is perhaps because Laing replaces the notion of 'existence' from the earlier work with that of 'experience'. And while 'existence' is neither a simple nor homogenous notion it does remain coherent throughout Laing's exposition, mostly because he confined it to the enclosed world of the individual and because it was mostly conceived within the phenomenological and existential framework. 'Experience' is very different. It has nothing to do with phenomenology as it is a concept that comes from the English empirical tradition. Laing understood it in many different ways and as an all-embracing concept for virtually all that happens between people. Furthermore, *Self and Others* does not have a continuous narrative or an exposition of a particular line of argument. Laing presents his thoughts in a series of statements which simply follow one another, paragraph after paragraph. When attempting to strip the contents of *Self and Others* to bare essentials we are left with a web of experiences of which some are private and some are public, some are communicated, some remain hidden.

The book is arranged in two parts. The first deals with different modalities of experience as they are played out within the individual's psychic life. The three modalities which are most often dealt with are dreaming, phantasizing, imagining. Through shifting from one to another, through playing off one against another we manage to avoid conflict, we pretend, elude, develop a masturbatory life. And we often get it wrong.

> The error is not so much of content, as of category. We are aware of the *content* of experience, but are unaware that it is illusion. We see the shadows, but take them for the substance. A closely related error of category is to confuse the *modality* of experience.
>
> (SO:38)

The last chapter of the first part, entitled 'The coldness of death', is a moving case of a woman whose imagining, phantasizing and dreaming blend into a psychosis. She was convinced that she was about to die.

> To her, her skin had a dying pallor. Her hands were unnaturally blue, almost black. Her heart might stop at any moment. Her bones felt twisted and in a powder. Her flesh was decaying.
>
> (SO:70)

As it turned out all these experiences were a sort of mapping over onto her body what she had witnessed in others. The colour of her skin was the same as that of her brother when he was dying of tuberculosis; the black and blue hands were just like her baby's face in a breath-holding attack; the stopping heart was her baby during her pregnancy when there had been anxiety about something going wrong; the twisted bones were the bones of her mother who had suffered from severe arthritis. The episode lasted five months and after she emerged from it she described it with the following: 'I seem to have been living in a metaphorical state. I wove a tapestry of symbols and have been living in it' (SO:73–74).

The second part of *Self and Others* concentrates on the fact that we attribute experiences to each other. Laing says that 'the investigation of who attributes what to whom, when, why and how is a science in itself' (SO:27). The possibilities of mystification, confusion, misunderstanding, false attributions are endless and the greater part of the book is an exploration of different modes in which humans become entangled. The headings of several chapters are forms of these entanglements: 'Complementary identity', 'Confirmation and disconfirmation', 'Collusion', 'False and untenable positions', 'Attributions and injunctions'. Behind this list lies an exposition of the endless ways in which we acquire false personalities, collude, drive each other crazy, and so forth. There is plenty of clinical material with which Laing supports his expositions and in addition he draws examples from two master investigators of psychological perfidy and violence – Sartre and Dostoyevsky. After going through a few examples from both of these writers Laing finishes with an example from *Crime and Punishment*. Just before the murder, Raskolnikov receives a long letter from his mother, and this letter is dissected by Laing. This dissection is a real *tour de force*. Laing shows how Raskolnikov's mother presents him with a series of statements which contradict each other, entangling him in a really evil web. Laing comments: 'To move in any direction sanctioned by the letter, or to sustain consistently one position among the numerous incompatibilities in the letter, requires him to be defined within the framework of the letter as spiteful and evil' (SO:172). Laing ends his analysis with the following:

> The letter as it were explodes in him. He is shattered as one says. Dostoyevsky gives us some of the débris. Napoleon in his imagination, a little boy in his dream, a murderer in fact. Finally, through his crime and punishment, he wins through to Sonia, and Dunya finds happiness with his friend Razumihkin. His mother dies mad.

> (SO:173)

These are, bar the appendix, the concluding words of *Self and Others*. On reading this grim ending, and all the preceding analyses, one realizes that the book would be more appropriately entitled 'Self *Against* Others' as that is what the 'and' in Laing's analysis stands for.

III

The subject matter of *Self and Others*, particularly the second part, was linked with research into interpersonal communication which Laing had been carrying out at the Tavistock Clinic. This research converged largely with studies on family interactions which had already been under way in the United States and, like everyone else in this field, Laing was indebted to a pioneering study in Palo Alto, California, reported in a paper written by Gregory Bateson, Jay Haley, Don Jackson and John Weakland, 'Towards a Theory of Schizophrenia'. It was published in 1956. This paper of twenty-odd pages introduced the concept of the 'double bind'. It has been immensely influential, and for good reasons, for it introduced a conceptual framework for investigation of human interactions which has proved very rich. In fact, so many subsequent studies of the complexities of family communications are based one way or another on the 'double bind' formulation, that it can be said to be as important to the researchers in this field as the notion of the unconscious is to psychoanalysts. It is worth going into some detail in presenting it for that reason alone but also because many of the ideas that make up the argument of Bateson and Co. can also be found in Laing's expositions.

The theoretical premise of the research of Bateson was that human communication takes place at different levels of abstraction. Direct speech, metaphor, humour, etc., are all different modes of communication. In order to clarify these differences he took recourse to Russell's theory of Logical Types. This states that there is a discontinuity between a class and its members as the term 'class' is on a different level of abstraction from the term 'member'. Class and member do not belong to the same Logical Type. Russell postulated a discontinuity between different Logical Types. However, human communication involves a complex capacity to move from one Logical Type to another, from one level of abstraction to another. Metaphor, deception, humour are all based on an interplay between these different levels. The way we situate ourselves within this communicational network is our identity. Bateson states that

> according to our thesis, the term 'ego function' is precisely *the process of discriminating communicational modes either within the self or between the self and others*.

(Bateson 1973:176)

Then Bateson applies this thesis to analyse pathological functioning:

The schizophrenic exhibits weakness in three areas of such function: (a) He has difficulty in assigning the correct communicational mode to the messages he receives from other persons. (b) He has difficulty in assigning the correct communicational mode to those messages which he himself utters or emits non-verbally. (c) He has difficulty in assigning the correct communicational mode to his own thoughts, sensations, and percepts.

(ibid.:176)

This observation led to the hypothesis that in his upbringing the schizophrenic must have been systematically subjected to a particular pattern of communication which led to this difficulty. From there followed the theory of the 'double bind'. Here are its main features.

The double bind is a particular set of exchanges that happen between two or more persons. The context in which the researchers studied it was the family. The child was designated as the 'victim' and the mother, or father, or both parents, as those who inflict the double bind. The experience has to be repeated, and so the theory that the authors propose is not a hypothesis of a single traumatic experience but an outcome of a prolonged repetitive experience. Its specific result is that the victim comes to expect the same experience happening again. The double bind consists of a few ingredients. The first is a *primary negative injunction*.

> This may have either of two forms: (a) 'Do not do so and so, or I will punish you' or (b) 'If you do not do so and so, I will punish you'. Here we select a context of learning based on avoidance of punishment rather than a context of reward seeking. There is perhaps no formal reason for this selection. We assume that the punishment may be either the withdrawal of love or the expression of hate or anger or – most devastating – the kind of abandonment that results from the parent's expression of extreme helplessness.

(ibid.:178)

To this the authors added a footnote explaining that their notion of punishment should be understood as a process which involves perceptual experience and in this sense goes beyond the notion of trauma. Then comes a *secondary negative injunction*.

> The second injunction conflicts with the first but it is not immediately recognized as it happens at a more abstract level. This secondary injunction is more difficult to describe than the primary

for two reasons. First, the secondary injunction is commonly communicated to the child by non-verbal means. Posture, gesture, tone of voice, meaningful action and the implications concealed in verbal comment may all be used to convey this more abstract message. Second, the secondary injunction may impinge upon any element of the primary prohibition. Verbalization of the secondary injunction may, therefore, include a wide variety of forms; for example, 'Do not see this as punishment'; 'Do not see me as the punishing agent'; 'Do not submit to my prohibitions'; 'Do not think of what you must not do'; 'Do not question my love of which the primary prohibition is (or is not) an example'; and so on. Other examples become possible when the double bind is inflicted not by one individual but by two. For example, one parent may negate at a more abstract level the injunctions of the other.

(ibid.:178–179)

The second injunction, like the first, is reinforced by punishments, threats to survival, etc. These two injunctions are in a conflict, a conflict which is difficult to recognize because the injunctions come at different levels of abstraction.

For the double bind situation to have an effect there needs to be a third obvious ingredient – the victim cannot escape. If a double bind situation involves the mother and the child then the possibility of escape naturally does not exist. But there are other ways of preventing escape such as emotional blackmail or capricious promises of love, for example.

Finally, after a prolonged double bind situation the victim (the child) begins to perceive the world in double-bind patterns and the complete set of ingredients is no longer necessary to precipitate panic, rage or any other learned response. This pattern may turn into a set of hallucinatory voices which act out the double bind again.

The most pronounced effect of a prolonged double bind situation is the inability to distinguish between different modes of communication and a regular way of dealing with this is what we see as pathology. Such a person may always think that there is something behind what is being said (a paranoid solution), or may laugh at and trivialize everything that is being said (a hebephrenic solution), or may simply withdraw from all communication (a catatonic solution). Needless to say, there are many other ways of coping with this.

A few other observations that the authors make are worth noting. Although the researchers did not seek to establish reasons for the mother's feelings towards the child, they suggest that the mother's relationship to her own mother may be at the source of it, or some other factor; for example, it could be that for some reason the child reminds the parent of his or her own childhood situation. But these important factors are not really examined as the paper only deals with the formal aspects of the communicational situation. Another interesting thing to note is that the authors think that a psychiatric hospital perpetrates the patient's double bind universe. As the hospital serves the interests of the staff just as much as, if not more than, those of the patients, the patients are continually subjected to confusing messages.

This lengthy presentation of the double bind theory serves primarily to help us come to grips with some of the problems that Laing's thinking presents. In some fundamental respects Laing follows the arguments of the Palo Alto group in full.[2] His concept of different modes of experience does not differ in any significant respect from the idea of different modes of communication in Bateson, particularly as Laing is concerned with the communicability of experiences. One thing that Laing does not do is analyse communication as taking place on different levels of abstraction and in this sense his writings do not have the formal rigour of Bateson's thought. Still, when he says that 'a closely related error of category is to confuse the *modality* of experience' (SO:38) he is basically repeating Bateson's thesis.

The differences are, however, more revealing. First of all, Bateson and his colleagues are very clear that they are investigating the formation of pathology, while Laing seems to see the entire arena of human communication as a network of double binds or other forms of mystification. There is another critical difference that ultimately leads their respective researches into quite different directions. There is something in Laing's analyses, some sort of assumption, though never spelt out, that there is a hypothetical 'pure' and 'uncontaminated' encounter. In the Introduction to *Interpersonal Perception*, a work that Laing prepared in collaboration with Phillipson and Lee, Laing writes:

> Over a hundred years ago Feuerbach effected a pivotal step in philosophy. He discovered that philosophy had been exclusively orientated around 'I'. No one had realized that the 'you' is as primary as the I. It is curious how we continue to theorize from an egoistic standpoint. In Freud's theory, for instance, one has the 'I' (ego), the 'over-me' (super-ego) and 'it' (id), but no *you*. Some philosophers, some psychologists, and more sociologists have

recognized the significance of the fact that social life is not made up of a myriad I's and me's only, but of you, he, she, we and them, also, and that the experience of you or he or them or us may indeed be as primary and compelling (or more so) as the experience of 'me'.

(IP:3)

Laing also refers to Martin Buber whose *I and Thou* made a great impression on him. 'Philosophically, the meaninglessness of the category "I" without its complementary category of "you" first stated by Feuerbach, was developed by Martin Buber' (IP:4). Laing declares an intention to produce a Feuerbach-influenced picture of social interactions, this much is clear, but throughout his lengthy expositions the 'You' never quite emerges, only the infernal 'Other' à la Sartre. And yet, although the 'You' never emerges it seems to operate as an ideal, as though there could be some encounter where the modalities of experience did not become confused and mutual recognition could take place. Just as in *The Divided Self* there was an 'authentic self', now one can posit an 'authentic encounter', though in actuality it never really happens.

That is not Bateson's position. To him *all* communication involves a breaching of Russell's logical discontinuities. In an earlier paper Bateson comments, 'if human thought and communication always conformed to the ideal, Russell would not – in fact could not – have formulated the ideal' (Bateson 1973:153). And the fact that we constantly mix different logical orders in our communication, that we change emphasis between different modes, shift from direct communication to meta-communication, is not the sign of the failings of communication but the source of its richness. It is no coincidence that although Bateson is best known for his studies on the pathological forms of communication, in fact his favourite examples in which communicational modes are mixed up, so to speak, are humour and play. The difference between playfulness with words and the 'word-salad' of schizophrenese does not lie in its content, as both may appear virtually the same, but in the fact that in the case of the latter there is no awareness of the unusualness of the utterances. Bateson refers to these as 'unlabelled metaphors'.

To illustrate this point with a clinical case, we can return to *The Divided Self*. There Laing analyses an exchange that takes place between Kraepelin and a patient. The doctor asks questions which are exasperating – the patient is asked where he is, or what his name is. He responds to this with a torrent which Kraepelin considers meaningless.

Laing proceeds to show that if we understand the situation in which the patient finds himself all his utterances make sense. In making sense of what the patient is saying Laing not only analyses what is going on but also 'labels' the patient's communications. 'Surely he is carrying on a dialogue between his own parodied version of Kraepelin, and his own defiant rebelling self' (DS:30). Kraepelin did not spot this, but we may ask: was the patient aware of how complex his response was? Bateson would probably doubt it.

IV

The different analyses of interpersonal communication, within couples and in families, make up the bulk of Laing's writings. He never doubted that only through the understanding of these could he arrive at a comprehensive 'science of persons'. This was, in fact, the opening argument of *The Divided Self*, but as the book developed it became an existential study of the 'inner world' of the psychotic. Thereafter, throughout his various attempts at defining a 'science of persons', there is always a new method. At the end of *Self and Others* Laing put in an appendix, 'A notation for dyadic perspectives', in which he presents his attempt to render human exchanges in a logical form. The notation is simple. For example p signifies the own person, $p \rightarrow p$ signifies the way the person sees him/herself, $p \rightarrow o$ the way the person perceives the other. With an addition of four more signs > better than, : compared to, $\equiv$ equivalent to, and $\not\equiv$ not equivalent to, Laing hopes to create a shorthand which would enable him to write in an abbreviated form the nature of exchanges that take place between people. So, for example, a statement 'I suppose he thinks that I love him' could be rendered as $o \rightarrow (p \rightarrow (o \rightarrow p))$, or, the king, p, wants someone to be frank and honest so that he can *really* know what the other thinks of him, $p \rightarrow (o \rightarrow p) \equiv o \rightarrow p$. This kind of notation comes up in several of Laing's writings; in *Interpersonal Perception* which Laing researched with two other therapists from the Tavistock, Phillipson and Lee, we even find a questionnaire to be used to test the concordance/discordance within married couples, a kind of test one would expect to find in a marriage guidance clinic.

The intrinsic value of this notation is not obvious, except, perhaps, that it makes comparative studies easier. It is doubtful, however, if it is possible to give justice to the variety of experience by reducing it to a single 'p' or 'o'. Another thing is that these attempts seem to be going in the opposite direction from the phenomenological descriptions that we find in *The Divided Self*: anyone who has ever dipped into any form of this kind of notation will know how differently it reads. This codified shorthand may be more scientific but is as estranging as the psychiatric jargon which Laing so persuasively argued against. One commentator referred to this as a 'loveless talk of a loveless reality' (Jacoby 1975:145).

In another attempt to render the interpersonal communication and perception intelligible, Laing published the little book *Knots* (1970), in which the spirals of misunderstandings (an image that comes up frequently in Laing's writings) are presented in an epigrammatic form.

Jack does not see something.
Jill thinks Jack does see it.
Jack thinks Jack does see it and Jill does not.
Jill does not see herself what
    she thinks Jack does see.

Jack tells Jill
    what Jack thinks Jill does not see.
Jill realizes
    that,
        if Jack thinks
            Jill does not see *that*,
            which Jill thinks she does,
        Jack does not see
            what Jill thought
                Jack saw.

                                                (K:65)

Whichever way we look we are always lost in a myriad of endless spirals.

V

One of the reasons that the Feuerbachian and Buberian 'You' never emerges is that Laing is most of all driven by a determination to pin down the sources of violence and alienation. An inspiration for this he found in Sartre. Laing always admired Sartre; *Being and Nothingness* influenced a great deal of the thinking which is behind *The Divided Self*. In 1961, the year of the publication of *Self and Others*, Sartre issued *Critique de la Raison Dialectique*. In this work Laing came across a way of approaching the subject of violence that he found very persuasive. He was so fascinated by the work that within four years of its appearance in France he produced a condensed presentation of it to the English reader, together with other works of Sartre from that period (in tandem with David Cooper). This was the book entitled *Reason and Violence. A Decade of Sartre's Philosophy. 1950–1960.*

The message is grim. The resources are scarce and there is not enough to go around. Therefore, the human environment is suffused with fear, anxiety and mistrust. The Other is a rival in the world defined by scarcity, the Other is excess, redundant; the Other is a contra-man, the anti-man belonging to another species. 'We are an intelligent flesh-eating human species, who understands and thwarts human intelligence, and whose end is the destruction of man' (RV:114). Man is a bundle of interiorized fantasies. He interiorizes the sense of scarcity which generates fear. This fear of scarcity lies at the heart of group bonding, it leads to the divisions between Us and Them. We are so filled with these structures that genuine reciprocity is impossible.

Abstract, pure, immediate reciprocity is ruptured, therefore, by interiorized scarcity. Need and scarcity determine the Manicheistic basis of action and morals. Violence and counter-violence are perhaps contingencies, but they are contingent necessities, and the imperative consequence of any attempt to destroy this inhumanity is that in destroying in the adversity the inhumanity of the contra-man, I can only destroy in him the humanity of man, and realize in me his inhumanity, my aim is to destroy his freedom – it is an alien force *de trop*. As long as scarcity remains our destiny, evil is irremediable, and this must be the basis to our ethic. The negative unity of interiorized scarcity in the dehumanization of reciprocity is re-exteriorized for us all in the unity of the world as common field of our oppositions, as the contradictory unit of multiple contradictory totalizations, and this unity we in turn re-interiorize in new negative unity. We are united by the fact of living in the whole world as defined by scarcity.

(RV:114–115)

This is not easy to understand, mostly because Laing's exposition reduces Sartre's 750-page volume to a tenth of its length. What matters most about Laing's attraction to Sartre is that he found there an approach in which human violence is at one and the same time seen as reverberating in the individual and as contributing to a group formation. I destroy the other but this destructiveness is also the foundation of the 'We'.

At the preliminary level a group is a collection of solitudes bound together by some external aim. Such a group is called a 'series'. It can be any group, a bus queue, for example.

The persons in a serial group are further characterized by their interchangeability. They are identical in their separation. All the members of the bus queue have a future object in common. In so far as this is so, each is the same as the other. Each is the same as the other in a further respect, in that, as well as identity in interchangeability, and separation, there is identity as alterity: the other that each is for the other is the same. Each is one too many.

A material object, the bus, determines the serial order, since there may not be room for all. Each is *redundant* for the other. It is impossible, however, to decide who specifically is redundant on any *a priori* basis, or by any intrinsic qualities of the individual. In the series alterity is unmitigated, as it were. Each is other for the other in so far as he is other. No one possesses in himself the reason for his ordinal position in the serial order. Each is identical to the other in so far as he is made, by the others, an other acting on the others.

(RV:122–123)

It is amazing how much one can read into a bus queue, but the line of argument is clear enough: a 'series' is a collection of individuals held together by some external aim. Every group has a serial component to it.

But a group as a 'series' is not stable. Once the external reason for its coming together disappears, so does the group. The group's cohesion depends on its internal mechanics, it has to become a bonded group. The bond is formed around a 'pledge'. This pledge, though it is not necessarily articulated, forms the sense of membership, ensures that no-one will betray the group and, most of all, controls the terror which each member of the group has interiorized.

The encounter with Sartre's thought gave Laing a new way of studying group dynamics and the first application of this Sartrean method comes in a paper published in 1962 in *New Left Review* entitled 'Series and Nexus in the Family' (reprinted, with some modifications, in *The Politics of Experience* (1967)). Like every other group, a family has some characteristics of a 'series'. One instance would be when the members of the family have little concern for each other except that they concern themselves with what the others, the neighbours, for example, say or think of them. But a family can also show the other type of bonding based on a pledge. Laing will call this type of a family a 'nexal' family.

> A family can act as gangsters, offering each other mutual protection against each other's violence. It is a reciprocal terrorism, with the offer of protection-security against the violence that each threatens the other with, and is threatened by, if anyone steps out of line.
>
> (PE:75)

Such a view of a family may seem somewhat shocking but Laing was often prone to expressing himself in extreme terms. On another occasion he describes such a family in a more straightforward and recognizable way.

> A child born into such a group is born into the rights-obligations, duties, loyalties, rewards-punishments, already in existence, and much of his or her childhood training is necessarily taken up with parental techniques of inducing the interiorization of this whole system.
>
> (SMF:181)

The period at the Tavistock Clinic was for Laing a period of intensive research. One of his projects was the study of communication in families where one of its members, a child, was diagnosed schizophrenic. The result of this work was published as *Sanity, Madness and the Family* and was co-authored by Aaron Esterson. Here we find a convergence of the influence of Bateson and other family researchers and of Sartre. Laing and Esterson set out to show that within the particular communication pattern of the family the behaviour of a diagnosed psychotic can be rendered intelligible. This line of thinking was already present in *The Divided Self* when Laing argued that the psychotic's comportment had to be studied within a 'behavioural field'. There he attempted to show that the psychotic is to some extent a function of the behaviour of the psychiatrist. Now this premise is carried over into the domain of the family. But it was not intended, as in many comparable studies, as a study on the aetiology of what goes under the heading of schizophrenia; in other words, it was not an attempt to prove that the family is the *cause* of a psychotic breakdown.

> We are interested in what might be called the family *nexus*, that multiplicity of persons drawn from the kinship group, and from others who, though not linked by kinship ties, are regarded as members of the family. The relationships of persons in a nexus are characterized by enduring and intensive face-to-face reciprocal influence on each other's experience and behaviour.
>
> (SMF:21)

Esterson and Laing selected from two London psychiatric hospitals eleven women who had been diagnosed schizophrenic by at least two senior psychiatrists. None of them suffered from any organic condition, such as epilepsy for example, and none of them had received more than fifty electroshocks in the year before the study began and no more than a hundred and fifty in all. Laing and Esterson interviewed the patients, the parents, the siblings. All of them were interviewed individually as well as jointly. Most of the interviews were tape-recorded. The authors present a selection of this material and provide a running commentary – highlighting what the interviewed are saying about each other, how they talk about the family's mad member, or how the respective members of the family construe their pasts. The commentary is completely devoid of any theoretical padding. Whatever theoretical stance there is, it is outlined in the Introduction, where, in fact, the authors eschew theoretical formulations. They state that their aim is to organize and present the material with as little interference on their part as possible. Typical of their stance are a few footnotes in which they acknowledge possible lines of interpretation which their material affords, but they no more than signal them, without taking them up. This would be one such typical comment:

> For reasons given in the introduction, we are limiting ourselves very largely to the transactional phenomenology of these family situations. Clearly, here and in every other family, the material we present is full of evidence of the struggle of each of the family members against their own sexuality. Maya without doubt acts on her own sexual experience, in particular by way of splitting, projection, denial, and so on. Although it is beyond the self-imposed limitation of our particular focus in this book to discuss these subjects, the reader should not suppose that we wish to deny or to minimize the person's *action on himself* (what psychoanalysts usually call defence mechanisms), particularly in respect of sexual feelings aroused towards family members, that is, in respect of incest.

> (SMF:42)

Sanity, Madness and the Family is a well-organized book. It draws the lines of its enquiry very clearly and it delivers what it promises to deliver. We find descriptions of families organized around a web of misunderstandings, false attributions, contradictions, mythologies. In some cases there is an almost complete incomprehension of what is happening to the patient or anyone else in the family. There is ultimately something intensely sad and disturbing in these pictures of devastation.

Laing and Esterson follow a method – they present in each instance a short clinical picture of the diagnosed schizophrenic, they give a brief background to the family history and give specific details of the interviewing that took place – but each family is treated individually with an attentiveness to its particular dynamics. This is a study of the highest quality. However, a few questions have been raised. The first one concerned the sample the authors chose. Why only women? Should not there have been some comparative study of male patients? But there was not any and the authors do not provide any explanation, they only state the fact that they chose eleven women for their study. On the one hand, it is difficult to see how it could have no significance, but on the other, it is just as difficult to read any particular significance into it. There does not seem to be any bias resulting from Laing's and Esterson's choice of material and so we are left with no clues as to why they selected this sample, giving the impression that this question never occurred to them. In a curious way this may be so much the better as it leaves the field open for others to use the material for further interpretations. Some feminists, for example, found these studies particularly helpful, especially since these family portraits centre mostly around the mother–daughter relationship.[3]

When *Sanity, Madness and the Family* first appeared it carried a sub-title: *Vol. I Families of Schizophrenics*. Evidently, the study was to be followed by a comparative one on 'normal' families. In the second edition the 'Vol.1' sub-title was dropped and the authors explained in the Introduction that 'after much reflection we came to the conclusion that a control group would contribute nothing to an answer to *our* question' (SMF:13). The authors went on to say that any comparison would be difficult since the data was not quantified (they did have it but chose not to present it because again they did not think it would have contributed much to their questions). Some have found this unsatisfactory and not in keeping with the standards of good methodology.[4] This is true, but, nevertheless, it is hard to disagree that a follow-up book on 'normal' families would contribute little if anything at all to the material presented in the first volume. Many years later Laing gave another explanation for giving up on the follow-up study. According to this one he could not bring himself to work on the second volume because the material was crushingly boring. All members of the family fitted, they had nothing to say, and Laing described these interviews as an endless drone; he found it difficult to stay awake when going through this material. 'It was like Samuel Beckett, reams and reams and reams of nothing. No one was particularly happy, no one was particularly up, no one had achieved anything or crashed in any way, they were just going along in their own way' (Mullan 1995:281). This answer, coming almost thirty years after the actual research was carried out, is quite witty and seductive but may well mean that Laing simply lost interest in the subject, rather than being a fair reflection on what was really happening in these families. Or it may well be that 'normal' families never really interested Laing, nor 'normality' of any sort, for that matter.

One criticism levelled at the book is particularly pertinent, pertinent because it meets the authors on their own ground. It has been pointed out that, although the aim of the book is to demonstrate the intelligibility of the schizophrenic's discourse, there is not one example of disjointed speech, no 'word-salad', no 'schizophrenese'. From the introductions to each of the eleven studies we can glean that at one point or another each of these women had a breakdown. They were deluded, they hallucinated, and, in brief, displayed all the kinds of behaviour that inevitably get diagnosed as psychotic. What they were like at those moments we do not find out. This is compared with the case of Julie in *The Divided Self* where Laing did analyse schizophrenic speech. And from there a weakness of Laing's and Esterson's approach is inferred.[5] This is not necessarily the case. Laing could present an analysis of Julie's broken language precisely because he had interviewed the family, so there is no reason why he could not have done the same later. We should also remember that word-salad is not that frequent and common and it is possible that it did not come up during the research. However, the framework adopted by Laing and Esterson does probably have certain limitations.

Laing always approached the problem of psychosis with a conviction that the psychotic's discourse can be made intelligible within the matrix of his/her communications. In this conviction he was consistent, and it goes back to the time of *The Divided Self*. There he presented his argument in order to reject psychoanalysis's use of the term 'unconscious'. To illustrate his point he discussed a case and gave a caricature of a psychoanalytical interpretation. He then stated that 'the central or pivotal issue in this patient's life is not to be discovered in her "unconscious"; it is lying quite open for her to see' (DS:56). Now, this statement is not so certain. The 'central or pivotal issue' in this patient's life may be lying quite 'open' for Laing to see, but not for her. What is visible to some is not visible to others. Probably all people experience the sense of a 'blind spot' which continually prevents them seeing things that others do. In a way, many of Laing's studies showed how these 'blind spots' contribute to breakdowns in communication. But in this instance he commits an error which he himself took great effort to expose – he *attributes* to her the visibility of the pivotal issue in her life, but he does not demonstrate it.

Laing places the psychotic experience within a 'behavioural field', to use his own term, that is, within the realm of the visible. He shows that the discourse of the psychotic can be made quite sensible when the phenomenon of the family is studied. All sorts of otherwise bizarre utterances can be deciphered as a set of exchanges between an overpowering mother and an ontologically insecure child, for example. The value of this cannot be overestimated as it renders intelligible many phenomena that would otherwise be considered as symptoms of a disease. It also explains a great deal about the mechanisms of a nuclear family. But although a great deal becomes intelligible, it does not mean that the pivotal issue of a psychotic experience is explained. Or it may be that this pivotal experience is made visible, but only to some, and not necessarily to those concerned.

According to one line of argument what is essential to a psychotic experience is precisely a hidden dimension. It operates constantly but it is not of the order of some 'organic' component or the instinctual realm of orthodox psychoanalysis. Some researchers who have been exploring the same schizophrenic family territory came to conclude that this invisible factor lies in the generation of the grandparents. This is not a mere addition of one more generation as it takes the problematic outside the immediate 'behavioural field'. It complicates the picture considerably and introduces new factors. The child is caught up in an unresolved conflict of the previous generation, between the mother and grandmother, for example. This conflict is not spoken of but in a crucial way it is always present. It may be that the child's existence, sometimes the very reason it was conceived, is to deal with this conflict. In such a scenario the selfhood of the child is eliminated as it silently and unknowingly carries the ballast which originates in the previous generation. The peculiarity of this ballast is that it encloses in a time which is regressive. The child's life is directed backwards, it exists in order to solve a conflict which comes from the past, it is enclosed in a temporality which precludes any possibility of having one's 'own time', and thus precludes life becoming an independent project.[6]

If we feed these remarks back to the material of *Sanity, Madness and the Family* we will not diminish in any way the book's value but we will conclude that the intelligibility of the schizophrenic's discourse can be made clear within the context of the family interactions only up to a point. But if the book does not answer this problem as fully as the authors hoped, then certainly the aim of presenting a family *nexus* was achieved. In this respect the book really works. Perhaps because of the low theoretical ballast and unobtrusive commentary the portraits of these families come across largely as self-portraits. Anyone who has ever worked with such families can recognize the particular flavour that Laing and Esterson bring home, even if it is difficult to pin down what exactly it is. Not all families of schizophrenics are like this, but the vast majority of them are, as are possibly quite a few so-called 'normal' families.

VI

The family, its dynamics and influences on our lives remained Laing's preoccupation. *The Politics of the Family*, a book that appeared in 1969, presents quite a different approach to his previous work. He no longer focuses on the schizophrenic family. Instead he grapples with the family as a general phenomenon. Sartrean dialectics does not play any role in these deliberations, either. Rather than study interactions within the family Laing is more concerned with a process which he calls 'mapping'. We internalize families as a whole, 'what is internalized is not objects as such but patterns of relationship by internal operations upon which a person develops an incarnate group structure' (PF:7). Thus we carry within us entire sets of rules, prohibitions, images that may have little to do with the physical family we are brought up in. We have in us a 'family'.

> The family here discussed is the family of origin transformed by internalization, partitioning, and other operations, into the 'family' and mapped back onto the family and elsewhere.
>
> (PF:3)

Laing was not alone in distinguishing between the actual physical family in which we are brought up and the internalized family. But it is not entirely clear what Laing means by the 'family of origin'. He seems to mean that there is an image of the family that we are born into, an image of the institution which is as old as our civilization. It permeates our society which in many of its structures repeats the family patterns.

Through continuous mapping and re-mapping we merge the two families – the 'family of origin' and the actual family. The actual family is relatively easy to leave; it is harder, but still possible, to leave behind most of the psychological and emotional baggage that the family has equipped us with; but it is impossible to shake off the imprint of the family altogether. Both the 'family of origin' and the family we actually live in make sure, in tandem, that we learn what the society wants of us, that we turn out 'normal'. By the time we are officially grown-up we are already done for:

> One is expected to be capable of passion, once married, but not to have experienced too much passion (let alone acted upon it) too much before. If this is too difficult, one has to pretend first not to feel the passion one really feels, then, to pretend to passion one does *not* really feel, and pretend that certain passionate upsurges of resentment, hatred, envy, are unreal, or don't happen, or are something else. This requires false realizations, false de-realizations, and a cover-story (rationalization). After this almost complete holocaust of one's experience on the altar of conformity, one is liable to feel somewhat empty, but one can try to fill one's emptiness up with money, consumer goods, position, respect, admirations, envy of one's fellows for their business, professional, social success. These together with a repertoire of distractions, permitted or compulsory, serve to distract one from one's own distraction: and if one finds oneself overworked, under too great a strain, there are perfectly approved additional lines of defence, concoctions to taste of, narcotics, stimulants, sedatives, tranquillizers to depress one further so that one does not know how depressed one is and to help one to over-eat and over-sleep. And there are lines of defence beyond *that*, to electroshocks, to the (almost) final solution of simply removing sections of the offending body, especially the central nervous system. This last solution is necessary, however, only if the *normal social* lobotomy does not work, and chemical lobotomy has also failed.
>
> (PF:90–91)

With or without the help of Sartre Laing's message remained unforgiving.

VII

Various analyses of interpersonal perception, family life, group bonding, occupy a large proportion of Laing's writings but a coherent picture does not really emerge from these. Laing changed his position often and his avowed intention of presenting a complete theory of a 'science of persons' did not materialize.[7] It seems that at times he was carried away by the intensity of his emotions, which affected his analyses. His views concerning the family pertain to no more than a very particular type of family set-up and lack any appreciation of the developments and changes that the institution of the family underwent throughout history.[8] One could say that Laing's 'family' is a cardboard cut-out which gives us a skewed perspective. So, although Laing stated that his work was not intended to analyse the reasons for going insane, only the context in which insanity takes place, he is often remembered as one of those who put on the families the blame for their children's predicament.

In *The Politics of the Family* Laing recounts how he was once asked to give his opinion/diagnosis of a nine-year-old boy who had been giving trouble and consequently had been attending a Child Guidance Clinic. Laing uses this incident to argue the view that the family as a whole has to be understood. He describes how he went about setting up a meeting where most of the family members would be present. Why it should be done in this manner he explains convincingly in the following way:

> If one has 'a referral', say, from a hockey team, because the left back is not playing properly, one wouldn't think only of getting the left back round to one's office, taking a history, and giving a Rorschach. At least I hope not. One would also go to see how the team plays hockey. One would certainly get nowhere if one had no idea of hockey, and what games within games can be played through it.
>
> (PF:28)

One cannot argue with this line of reasoning but at the end of the case presentation Laing concludes that 'no one should see the boy if he did not wish to see anyone, but that someone should have sessions with Mrs Clark [the boy's mother] and her mother' (PF:28–29). Now, in this particular instance this may have indeed been the best course to take, but somehow, after reading all of Laing, one has the impression that he would almost invariably arrive at a similar conclusion. Laing was always sensitive to the role of the mother and this question was a fraught one for a whole generation of researchers. Mothers are incontestably powerful in the lives of small children and have been consequently blamed for almost everything – too much, too little, not loving enough, loving too much, unprotective, overprotective, etc., etc. The notion of the 'schizophrenogenic mother' entered the professional vocabulary. Fathers were at most accused of being absent. Laing never went so far as to actually single out mothers as the guilty ones. Whenever he was carried away by his rhetoric it was more the family as a whole that he attacked. This anti-family rhetoric was frequent enough to give the feeling that Laing indeed saw families as responsible for all the misery that fills psychiatric hospitals and other institutions.

Of all Laing's writings around this subject *Sanity, Madness and the Family* is by far the most helpful book. Although the slant is there – mothers receive far more attention than fathers – it is the most measured and has the least prejudice in it, mostly because there is the least of Laing's rhetoric in it. And out of it the one type of family that he had been scrutinizing, namely the middle-class nuclear family, has come through rather vividly, even if somewhat grimly.

NOTES

1 The concept of phantasy and unconscious phantasy has been reviewed by J. Laplanche and J.-B. Pontalis in *The Language of Psychoanalysis*. They note Susan Isaacs' introduction of the different spelling but think that it does not do justice to the complexity of Freud's position (Laplanche and Pontalis 1980:318).

2 It is not certain that Laing is 'following' Bateson's arguments as he may well have developed his ideas independently. It is remarkable, however, how similar they are.

3 For example Juliet Mitchell in *Psychoanalysis and Feminism* (Mitchell 1974).

4 See Sedgwick (1972) and Mitchell (1974).

5 This point was first raised by Sedgwick (1972:26).

6 These last few lines have been culled from François Roustang's quite exceptional chapter 'Towards a New Theory of Psychosis' which comes at the end of *Dire Mastery* (Roustang 1982:132–156). The psychoanalyst Gisela Pankow was probably the first to systematically work with the relation between the parents and grandparents of psychotics (Pankow 1983). It is also worth recalling that Bateson thought that the reason for putting a child in a perpetual double bind may lie in events that preceded the child's life.

   Laing did speak of previous generations in his later writings. He was well aware that we are born into a lineage that determines a great deal who we become, but his comments on this sometimes come across more like bewildered passive observations, without any theoretical value, and he never discussed this problem in the specific context of a psychotic experience.

   Families (of some kind or another, albeit *very* different from ours) have existed, say, for 100,000 years. We can study directly only a minute slice in the chain: three generations, if we are lucky. Even studies of three generations are rare. What patterns can we hope to find, when we are restricted to three out of at least 4,000 generations?

(PF:77)

7 Juliet Mitchell remarks that each attempt brings a new method and adds: 'one has at some point to ask: are these real beginnings, or so many false starts?' (Mitchell 1974:247).
8 See for example the work of Donzelot (1979).

Chapter 4

The dialectics of liberation

I

Throughout his career Laing was broadening his canvas. He began with the analysis of the wretched state of the psychotic. Then he dissected the realm of interpersonal dynamics, the family of the schizophrenic and the whole phenomenon of the family in general. From there Laing progressed to the macrosocial scale and before long he arrived at a conclusion that it is our society that is profoundly sick.

> In the last fifty years, we human beings have slaughtered by our own hands coming on for one hundred million of our species. We all live under constant threat of our total annihilation. We seem to seek death and destruction as much as life and happiness. We are as driven to kill and be killed as we are to let live and live. Only by the most outrageous violation of ourselves have we achieved our capacity to live in relative adjustment to a civilization apparently driven to its own destruction. Perhaps to a limited extent we can undo what has been done to us, and what we have done to ourselves. Perhaps men and women were born to love one another, simply and genuinely, rather than to this travesty that we can call love. If we can stop destroying ourselves we may stop destroying others. We have to begin by admitting and even accepting our own violence, rather than blindly destroying ourselves with it, and therewith we have to realize that we are as deeply afraid to live and to love as we are to die.
>
> (PE:64)

Laing was not alone in voicing such thoughts. Capitalist society continued as though it was not capable of learning lessons. Hardly had the wounds of the Second World War healed and we were at it again – Korea, Algiers, Vietnam, the Cold War and there was the Bomb to finish it off, once and for all. A palpable feeling of threat was in the air and in the early 1960s a broad front of opposition began to emerge marked by the appearance of several influential thinkers. Herbert Marcuse, the German philosopher from the Frankfurt School and much respected expert on Hegel, Marx and Freud, now teaching at the University of California, published *One-Dimensional Man* (1964) with a scathing attack on the new affluent society; Frantz Fanon's *The Wretched of the Earth* (1965) gave a devastating analysis of colonialism; Jules Henry analysed the state of American society, its values and the mindlessness of the modern education system in *Culture Against Man* (1962). There were others and their voice was beginning to be heard. Laing felt part of that movement.

In 1967, together with three other psychiatrists – Joseph Berke, David Cooper and Leon Redler – he organized in London the Congress of the Dialectics of Liberation, a two-week jamboree of assorted radical thinkers. Among those involved were Gregory Bateson, the Black leader Stokeley Carmichael, Herbert Marcuse and the beat poet Allen Ginsberg. Laing's address to the Congress, 'The Obvious', is for the most part an attack on the policies of the American government, on the Vietnam War, on the spiral of paranoia generated by endless mystifications to which the citizen of the developed world is subjected. The sweep of the address is wide, from American politics to the violence of psychiatry, from microsocial events to the war in Vietnam. Our world is a sham, we do not know any more who we can trust, who we can turn to. This was the one time when Laing was most explicit in his general social/political outlook. Other utterances, mostly in *The Politics of Experience*, were similar in content and tone, though they were only occasional. These are views which are of an obviously political nature but Laing never organized them within any coherent political thought. Although he felt strong discontent with the capitalist system he did not espouse the Marxist ideology, as would appear to be natural considering his general outlook. But, nevertheless, the New Left considered Laing to be part of its ranks. 'Ronald Laing must be accounted one of the main contributors to the theoretical and rhetorical armoury of the contemporary left' was one assessment (Sedgwick 1982:95).

Considering how many others in the same period were critical of the capitalist system without moving into a Marxist ideology, Laing's lack of conversion into radical politics is not that surprising. More surprisingly, although Laing had the reputation of being a severe critic of the psychiatric system, we will not find in his works any detailed analyses of how this system works, nothing about the structures of power which are behind the profession, the hospital, the pharmaceutical industry, and so forth. This came from others. At the same time that a broad front of radical thinking was forming, the first critiques of the psychiatric system began to appear. They became required reading and reached a wide audience. Amongst the first to appear, perhaps three made a particularly strong impression. Laing also knew them. The first was Erving Goffman's *Asylums*, published in 1961. Goffman, a university sociologist, spent a year in a mental hospital of over seven thousand inmates, employed as an assistant physical therapist. The lowly status of his position enabled him to mix closely with the patients and, although he did not sleep on the ward, he avoided social contacts with the staff, of whom only those from the top management knew the aim of his study. From this position Goffman could draw material for his study of the closed community of the hospital inmates. The hospital he considered a 'total institution', as are prisons, concentration camps, etc. In this exhaustive study, which consists of four long separate essays, Goffman shows how the hospital teaches patients their new role and how the patients learn to perceive themselves in their role. He also examines the differentiation between the staff and inmates, the rituals and ceremonies of these institutions. Goffman was responsible for introducing the concept of the 'career' of a hospital inmate and *Asylums* remains one of the most important studies on life inside mental hospitals.

The second important work was *The Myth of Mental Illness* by Thomas Szasz, which also appeared in 1961. It is nowhere as militant as the title might suggest. The bulk of it is taken up by the exposition of Szasz's 'Foundations of a Theory of Personal Conduct', which is the sub-title of the book. Szasz's social theories did not get much of an airing, but his biting critique of the practices of psychiatry has become very well known. Szasz argues that the term 'mental illness' is no more than a metaphor; 'minds can be "sick" only in the sense that jokes are "sick" or economies are "sick"' (Szasz 1972:275). We can speak of an illness of the brain but, despite tremendous efforts, no evidence that the inmates in hospitals suffer from any brain malfunctioning has been unearthed.[1] Szasz further argues that the metaphor of mental illness is used to persecute those whom the society finds undesirable. Psychiatry is an institution of oppression.

Other works followed and Szasz ceaselessly documented abuses of psychiatry. In *The Manufacture of Madness*, published in 1970, Szasz re-writes the history of psychiatry. According to this rendering psychiatry is not a new science beginning with Pinel and Samuel but a practice with a long lineage going back to the Inquisitio witch-hunting. Words such as 'Jew', 'witch', 'homosexual', 'Commu-nist', 'mentally ill' are interchangeable. Under the guise of a science, psychiatry is engaged in issues of a moral and political dimension. The argument was simple and Szasz never deviated from it; as the years went on he supplied endless examples to support it and Szasz's name has become a landmark. Szasz's argument is often referred to as the 'conspiratorial model of madness' and it has been defined thus:

> Schizophrenia is a *label* which some people pin on other people, under certain social circumstances. It is not an illness, like pneumonia. It is a form of alienation which is out of step with the prevailing state of alienation. It is a social fact and political event.
>
> (Siegler, Osmond and Mann 1972:101)

All anti-psychiatrists agreed with this view, at least to an extent.

On the wave of these denouncements of the hospital system an American sociologist, Rosenham, carried out an experiment aiming to see if any of these theses could be vindicated (Rosenham 1975). Eight volunteers entered twelve different hospitals as patients. The hospitals were in five different states on the West and East coasts of America. All these pseudopatients gained admission by simply arriving at the hospital and claiming that they were hearing voices. On being asked the nature of the voices they would say that the voices were unclear but the words that they could discern were 'empty', 'hollow' and 'thud'. The voice that was uttering these words was unfamiliar and of the same sex as the pseudopatient. This and the false name (in order to avoid ending up having a psychiatric record) were the only information that they provided which was not true. The personal and family histories were not distorted to fit the feigned 'illness', nor was any other information. As soon as they entered the ward they claimed that they were not hearing voices any more, were behaving normally, and asked to be released. All of them eventually were (the stay in the ward ranged from nine to fifty-two days) but each one of them left with a diagnosis of schizophrenia. During their stay they took notes on the life on the ward, at first secretly, then, on realizing that the staff did not take any notice, openly. (In some instances the staff did notice the writing and put it down in their records as 'writing behaviour', another symptom of their disease.) None of the staff spotted the pseudopatients as simulating although quite commonly the patients on the ward did. After the results of the experiment were published one hospital claimed that it could not have happened there. Rosenham declared he would repeat the experiment. In the subsequent three months, of the 193 patients admitted to the hospital forty-one were thought to be pseudopatients by one staff member, twenty-three by at least one psychiatrist, nineteen by a psychiatrist and one other staff member. No volunteers were sent there.

This experiment demonstrated two things. First, it showed that the psychiatric diagnosis is completely uncertain; the psychiatrists failed both when they were supposed to diagnose illness and when they were asked to detect malingerers. Second, it showed how difficult it was to get out of the hospital once the diagnosis was affixed.

The third work that made a great impact was Michel Foucault's *Madness and Civilization*. Foucault attempts to give us a reconstruction of how throughout history the understanding and response to madness developed, and how we have arrived at our modern conception of madness. The span that he covered stretches from the Middle Ages to the beginning of the nineteenth century.

The book's opening image is the leper house. For a few centuries leprosy was the scourge that swept through Europe and the leper house was part of the social landscape. When the Crusades ended the disease began to disappear and the vast structure set up to deal with it started to become redundant. Over the following few centuries, the emptying leper houses would be filled by the insane, taking on the role that the lepers once had. Foucault traces the differing attitudes to madness from the image of the Ship of Fools to the birth of a modern asylum. The mad were chained to walls, coerced into obedience, put to work, subjected to 'moral' improvement. The remarkable dimension about this analysis is the reinterpretation of the role of Pinel and Tuke, the two pioneers of modern psychiatry. They are best known for releasing the mad from their chains and instituting psychiatry without physical constraint. These first experiments are hailed as the dawn of a new enlightened approach. Foucault offers a quite different view: it was possible to take the chains off only after madness was mastered by Reason; it was only possible after the essence of the mad person's discourse had been smothered by Reason's silence. The birth of psychiatry, as we know it today, is the breakdown of dialogue between Reason and Unreason. The psychiatric hospital is the City of Reason which borrows some of its repressive measures from the penal system but most of all invents its own code which is personified by the Doctor. He is at the same time the Father, the Judge, the Family and the Law. This paragraph from Foucault's introduction to the book sums up his position very well:

In the serene world of mental illness, modern man no longer communicates with the madman: on one hand, the man of reason delegates the physician to madness, thereby authorizing a relation only through the abstract universality of disease; on the other, the man of madness communicates with society only by the intermediary of an equally abstract reason which is order, physical and moral constraint, the anonymous pressure of the group, the requirements of conformity. As for a common language, there is no such thing; or rather, there is no such thing any longer; the constitution of madness as a mental illness, at the end of the eighteenth century, affords the evidence of a broken dialogue, posits the separation as already effected, and thrusts into oblivion all those stammered, imperfect words without fixed syntax in which the exchange between madness and reason was made. The language of psychiatry which is a monologue *about* madness, has been established only on the basis of such a silence.

(Foucault 1971:x–xi)

In a short passage Foucault also makes some interesting comments on the birth of psychoanalysis. He notes that although the patient is no longer imprisoned in the hospital, and his speech has been freed, the psychoanalyst has retained all that is invested in the personage of the Doctor. Consequently, psychoanalysis may perhaps unravel some structures of madness but ultimately it cannot hear the voice of Unreason (ibid.:278).

Foucault's work has been immensely influential for the three theses that he argued: first, that the meaning of madness has changed in history – with which all historians now agree; second, that there once was a period when Reason and Unreason were in dialogue – which is historically doubtful but opens an important theoretical perspective; and third, that Reason is a face of Power – thus putting the question of Power at the centre of the problem of psychiatry.

II

The works of Goffman, Szasz and Foucault had a great influence on Laing's thinking. But one voice, rarely mentioned, which seems to have been of capital importance to Laing, is that of Antonin Artaud.

Artaud, a writer, theatre theoretician, actor, was an outstanding figure of the avant-garde in Paris in the 1920s and 1930s. In 1937 he suffered a breakdown and ended up in a psychiatric hospital where he spent the next nine years. It was an appalling experience. During the time of internment Artaud was subjected to, amongst other 'treatments', a series of at least sixty electroshocks. What the stay in the care of psychiatrists did to him can be gauged from photographs of Artaud taken immediately before and at the end of his psychiatric career – the earlier show a handsome man in his mid-thirties, the photographs from a decade later show a ravaged face of a man one would have thought was well into his sixties. The difference is truly shocking.

Artaud vented his hatred of psychiatry in one of his best-known essays, 'Van Gogh, The Man Suicided by Society'. It is an extraordinary piece of writing which mixes beautiful and insightful descriptions of Van Gogh's paintings with a savage indictment of psychiatry. Artaud wrote it after a great exhibition of Van Gogh's works in Paris but the immediate reason that triggered it off was an article by a psychiatrist describing Van Gogh as a degenerate. Artaud's response was couched in relentlessly uncompromising terms:

> In comparison with the lucidity of Van Gogh, which is a dynamic force, psychiatry is no better than a den of apes who are themselves obsessed and persecuted and who possess nothing to mitigate the appalling states of anguish and human suffocation but a ridiculous terminology.
>
> (Artaud 1976:484)

This is still mild in comparison to what Artaud had to add. He claimed that Van Gogh committed suicide because he was in the hands of psychiatrists, it was they who pushed him into killing himself. Why? Because 'there is in every living psychiatrist a repulsive and sordid atavism that makes him see in every artist, every genius he comes across, an enemy' (ibid.:493). No, it is not surprising that Van Gogh committed suicide while in the care of a psychiatrist. In fact, according to Artaud, Van Gogh killed himself after a conversation with Dr Gachet, the psychiatrist in question. And Artaud knows what it is like to talk to a psychiatrist:

> I myself spent nine years in an insane asylum and I never had the obsession of suicide, but I know that each conversation with a psychiatrist, every morning at the time of his visit, made me want to hang myself, realizing that I would not be able to cut his throat.
>
> (ibid.:497)

Artaud did not consider himself an individual victim. The existence of psychiatry is a reflection on our society. The society is sick and it cannot tolerate the voice of the madman.

Things are going badly because sick consciousness has a vested interest right now in not recovering from its sickness.

This is why a tainted society has invented psychiatry to defend itself against the investigations of certain superior intellects whose faculties of divination would be troublesome.

(ibid.:483)

and

psychiatry was born of the vulgar mob of creatures who wanted to preserve the evil at the source of illness and who have thus pulled out of their own inner nothingness a kind of Swiss guard knife to cut off at its root that impulse of rebellious vindication which is at the origin of genius.

(ibid.:492)

Strong words that take one aback. It is easy to dismiss Artaud as a raving madman and, in fact, there would not be many psychiatrists who would hesitate to judge Artaud insane on the strength of this essay alone. But Artaud himself was well aware that he had often been very sick. He suffered immensely, he was evidently mad, in a manner of speaking. It may well be that one has to be in such a state to write with such intensity. But this does not invalidate Artaud's discourse. There is enough there to suggest that it was not a work of a deranged mind. His analyses of Van Gogh's situation, of his relationship to his brother Theo, of the act of painting, of the relation between madness and society, are penetrating. It is a voice which, although not comfortable, has to be listened to and what it has to say in general is that society is such that it will not tolerate the likes of Van Gogh, Baudelaire, Poe, Gérard de Nerval, Nietzsche, Kierkegaard, Holderlin, Coleridge. Our society is too sick for such men. They suffer, but psychiatry, designated by society to treat them, has nothing to offer. Instead it perpetrates society's own sickness.

'Van Gogh, The Man Suicided by Society' is the only work Artaud lived to see given some official recognition – in 1947 it was awarded the Prix Saint-Beuve for the best essay published in that year.

III

To the new theoreticians of madness Artaud was an emblematic figure, the one where madness and genius came together. Foucault had him very much in mind when he spoke of the breakdown in the discourse between Reason and Unreason in *Madness and Civilization*. Laing also knew Artaud's essay. He never referred to it specifically but he had come across it very early on and apparently it made a great impression on him.[2] Therefore the similarity of some of Laing's views and of Artaud's is not a coincidence. Laing, of course, never expressed himself in such a forceful way, and he could not have. After all, he did not spend nine years as a patient in a psychiatric hospital, he was a psychiatrist himself. But as years progressed his views, and some of his rhetoric, came close to those of Artaud.

In the Preface to the Pelican edition of *The Divided Self* written four years after the book had been first published Laing wrote:

> I am still writing in this book too much about Them and too little about Us . . . A man who says that men are machines may be a great scientist. A man who says he *is* a machine is 'depersonalized' in psychiatric jargon . . . A little girl of seventeen in a mental hospital told me she was terrified because the Atom Bomb was inside her. That is a delusion. The statesmen of the world who boast and threaten that they have Doomsday weapons are far more dangerous, and far more estranged from 'reality' than many of the people on whom the label 'psychotic' is affixed.
>
> (DS:11–12)

Laing no longer wants to write about the state of psychosis from the other side, from the side which passes judgement and considers itself radically other than the condition it describes. The classical psychiatrists – Kraepelin and Bleuler and the next, more enlightened generation such as Jaspers or Bleuler's son Manfred – held that there was a radical discontinuity between madness and sanity. With this Laing disagrees.

> Thus I would wish to emphasize that our 'normal' 'adjusted' state is too often the abdication of ecstasy, the betrayal of our true potentialities, that many of us are only too successful in acquiring a false self to adapt to false realities.
>
> (DS:12)

After the period of research into the vagaries of interpersonal communication Laing returned to the question of psychosis, but with a difference. Instead of analysing reasons which lead to behaviour described as psychotic Laing suggests that perhaps a psychotic's discourse may also carry a different dimension. It is not any more the question of trying to make sense of the unusual psychotic utterances in the matrix of 'normal' communication; now Laing is proposing that a psychotic's experience may be an opening to that realm of ecstasy which our normality has banished from our lives. Most that Laing wrote about this is contained in two chapters of *The Politics of Experience*, 'Transcendental experience' and 'A ten-day voyage'. In 'Transcendental experience' Laing states:

> [the madman] often can be to us, even through his profound wretchedness and disintegration, the hierophant of the sacred. An exile from the scene of being as we know it, he is an alien, a stranger, signalling to us from the void in which he is foundering, a void which may be peopled by presences that we do not even dream of. They used to be called demons and spirits, and they used to be known and named. He has lost his sense of self, his feelings, his place in the world as we know it. He tells us he is dead. But we are distracted from our cosy security by this mad ghost that haunts us with his visions and voices that seem so senseless and of which we feel impelled to rid him, cleanse him, cure him.
>
> (PE:109–110)

This could have been written by Artaud, though he would have probably spat it out with more venom. And, as it was Laing's habit to quote prominent psychiatrists and then re-interpret their material, Laing quotes below on the same page an account of a patient from Karl Jaspers's *General Psychopathology* (1962). The patient describes an experience of penetrating the 'other world' while in a psychotic state. It is quite a long account where the patient describes how he came to know the world of spirits and the 'source of life', how he experienced the need to enter death. When he recovered he felt that the experience was of great value to him. Jaspers admits that this account cannot be dismissed as a chaotic jumble but still sees it as the morbid mind at work. Laing, by contrast, considered this to be a lucid description of a spiritual quest.

Another source from which Laing drew support for his views was the upsurge of autobiographical accounts of the experience of madness. They often suggested (though not all of them) that what psychiatrists take to be a delusional system is in fact a way of getting in touch with a realm which would be otherwise unavailable to them. All these accounts convey the sense of danger and risk that the state of psychosis puts one in, but for those who emerged from it it was enhancing as well as frightening.[3]

Laing also contributed to this literature. In 'A ten-day voyage', the second pertinent chapter from *The Politics of Experience*, he presented a tape-recorded account of a breakdown which lasted ten days and which had all the hallmarks of a voyage into another reality. The story came from his friend, a sculptor, Jesse Watkins, who recounted to Laing the incident twenty-seven years after it had taken place.

It began suddenly without any apparent warning. From one moment to the next Watkins felt that he was going back in time, as though into some previous existence. He started talking gibberish. This behaviour alarmed his wife, she called an ambulance and he was whisked off to a hospital. While there he was given sedatives and at one point he was put in a padded cell but somehow all this did not hinder what he was going through. It lasted ten days. During this time he experienced the regression of time, the sense of the death of his ego, and, although not a religious person, neither before nor since, he experienced the Stations of the Cross. The voyage ended just as suddenly as it began: '[I decided] that I had to stop this business going on because I couldn't cope with it any more' (PE:131). He refused further medication, the doctor consented and that was the end of the matter. It was the only time that he experienced anything like this and he would not want to repeat it: 'I'd be afraid of entering it again' (PE:132). But, although it was frightening it was also enriching.

> When I came out of hospital . . . I suddenly felt that everything was so much more real that it – than it had been before. The grass was greener, the sun was shining brighter, and people were more alive, I could see them clearer. I could see the bad things and the good things, and all that. I was much more aware.
>
> (PE:136)

This account of a psychotic breakdown, together with the other accounts that had been appearing in print, led Laing to conclude that there are certain elements in the psychotic breakdown that suggest that it is an experience which is not only a disintegration but may also be a way of coming in contact with some other reality. Are we right in considering such states as necessarily pathological? Laing's answer is quite clear – while there is undeniable suffering we should start becoming open to the other dimensions that the psychotic experience may sometimes present.

This line of reasoning provoked quite an extraordinary response. Laing became really beyond the pale. It was one thing to analyse the schizophrenic behaviour within the existential tradition, as he did in *The Divided Self*, it was also perfectly in order to suggest that something goes wrong in schizophrenic families, but it was quite another thing to suggest that the psychotic is a seeker of some mystical realm which is not accessible to 'normal' beings.

The intensity of the reaction to this part of Laing's work was quite out of proportion to what Laing seemed to be stating. Views that he never held were attributed to him; views that he did hold were exaggerated, taken out of context and given an altogether new meaning. He was, and is, said to be romanticizing madness. He was encouraging people to go mad as this would enrich their lives. And yet, going through Laing's writings it is surprising to see how little there is, if anything, to justify these reactions. Whenever he wrote on the subject there always seemed a degree of caution and warning.[4] In one of the comments to the 'voyage' of Jesse Watkins he remarks: 'Such an experience can be extremely confusing and may end disastrously' (PE:128). These following quotes seem to be characteristic of Laing's attitude:

> Madness need not be all breakdown. It *may* also be breakthrough. It is potentially liberation and renewal as well as enslavement and existential death.
>
> (PE:110, italics added)

or

> *Some* psychotic people have transcendental experiences . . . I am not saying, however, that psychotic experience necessarily contains this element more manifestly than sane experience.
>
> (PE:112, italics added)

and

> Some people labelled schizophrenic (not all, and not necessarily) manifest behaviour in words, gestures, actions (linguistically, prelinguistically and kinetically) that is unusual. Sometimes (not always and not necessarily) this unusual behaviour (manifested to us, the others, as I have said, by sight and sound) expresses, wittingly or unwittingly, unusual experiences that the person is undergoing. Sometimes (not always and not necessarily) these unusual experiences that are expressed by unusual behaviour appear to be part of a potentially orderly, natural sequence of experiences.
>
> (PE:102)

Laing goes on to add that 'treatment' often interrupts this natural sequence of experiences. Now, it is difficult to imagine a statement more hedged with caution. At no point did Laing lose sight of the fact that a breakdown is also 'enslavement and existential death'. So why should these views provoke such a strong reaction? In part this was because Laing's views were conflated with those of David Cooper, his collaborator in *Reason and Violence*. All of Cooper's subsequent writings are far more unrestrained than Laing's. His views on the family and the relation between mother and child were at times excessive, and Cooper really saw the mentally ill as part of the vanguard in the fight against oppression, a position that Laing never adopted.[5] Their views differed in many other respects but in the popular perception they were saying the same. Even some serious commentators approached them completely blind to the obvious divergencies of their views.[6]

It should also be noted that Laing was not the first to have the idea that a psychotic breakdown may also be a healing process. In some respects the idea that people need to break down is almost a pretty standard psychotherapeutic attitude. They need to regress, to cut through their restrictive defences, in order to move on, to change, to heal themselves, but maybe with the difference that this breakdown is meant to happen tidily, within the confines of the analytic space. Laing has something else in mind, and a full expression and clear articulation of this view of psychosis was articulated earlier, by Gregory Bateson, the 'double bind' theoretician. In the Introduction to a nineteenth-century account of a psychosis, *Perceval's Narrative*, which he edited, he had this to say:

> It would appear that once precipitated into psychosis the patient has a course to run. He is, as it were, embarked upon a voyage of discovery which is only completed by his return to the normal world, to which he comes back with insights different from those of the inhabitants who never embarked on such a voyage. Once begun, a schizophrenic episode would appear to have as definite a course as an initiation ceremony – a death and rebirth – into which the novice may have been precipitated by his family life or by adventitious circumstances, but which in its course is largely steered by endogenous process.
>
> In terms of this picture, spontaneous remission is no problem. This is only the final and natural outcome of the total process. What needs to be explained is the failure of many who embark upon this voyage to return from it. Do these encounter experiences either in family life or in institutional care so grossly maladaptive that even the richest and best organized hallucinatory experience cannot save them?
>
> (Bateson 1974:xiii–xiv)

We cannot go here into discussing how Bateson progressed from the 'double bind' theory of psychosis to this apparently quite different conception.[7] We may remark, however, that Bateson was quite familiar with initiation ceremonies from his extensive field work as an anthropologist, before he was involved in the field of psychiatry.[8] What matters most here is how similar, if not virtually identical, is this formulation to Laing's. And it was no coincidence. Laing knew Bateson's work, in fact he also quotes the above passage in the chapter 'The schizophrenic experience' in *The Politics of Experience*; he never claimed priority for these views.

So Laing thought that psychosis need not be viewed as just a sickness. He considered psychiatry to be a science of the alienated 'normality', a representative of our alienated world, therefore an inhuman theory, and 'an inhuman theory will inevitably lead to inhuman consequences' (PE:45). He not only thought that psychiatry was an alienated theory, that its practices were founded on violence and that this violence continued. He also viewed the world we live in as characterized by alienation; as far as he could see our society has become sick and estranges us from the sacred.

None of these views were particularly new; all this could be put together without even mentioning Laing. Others were saying much the same. But perhaps the fact that one would have to bring in several writers to say this while Laing was saying it *all* is what irked so much. And, no small matter, there was also the *way* in which he was saying it:

Much human behaviour can be seen as unilateral or bilateral *attempts* to eliminate experience . . . As adults, we have forgotten most of our childhood, not only its contents but its flavour; as men of the world we hardly know of the existence of the inner world . . . This state of affairs represents an almost unbelievable devastation of our experience. There is empty chatter about maturity, love, joy, peace . . . What we call 'normal' is a product of repression, denial, splitting, projection, introjection and other forms of destructive action on experience. It is radically estranged from the structure of being . . . The condition of alienation, of being asleep, of being unconscious, of being out of one's mind, is the condition of normal man.

(PE:22–24)

This kind of talk did not endear Laing to his fellow professionals.

Within Laing's own parameters these views are coherent and throughout consistent. Laing had an immense empathy with mental suffering, evident from his many case discussions. Whenever he ventured into the problems of interpersonal violence he never drew his examples from the behaviour of the insane but from 'normal' people, either imaginary (Jill and Jack, or characters from Dostoyevsky and Sartre), or real (the mothers, fathers, brothers and sisters of schizophrenics). Laing makes a plea on behalf of madness: it is the mad who are the oppressed. Right from the beginning Laing appealed to their 'inner' quality. In *The Divided Self* it was the true self that disappears under the false self systems. In the later writings he despaired at the non-existence of this true self in 'ordinary' people. In the same context Laing found an unusual way of praising Freud:

> The relevance of Freud to our time is largely his insight and, to a considerable extent, his *demonstration* that the *ordinary* person is a shrivelled, desiccated fragment of what a person can be.
>
> (PE:22)

At the same time that he was despairing about the state of 'normality' Laing was fascinated by the quality of some of the psychotic experiences. But in pointing out a difference he fell into an inconsistency. The true, the authentic, resides in the 'inner' self, or in the transcendental; all that makes up the muck takes place between people. To put it differently, Laing sought to establish a 'science of persons' in analysing the way they relate, but the absolute Truth, according to him, resides in the inner self, albeit a self that expands into a transcendental realm. It will not take long before one will discover that this scheme of things leads into a cul-de-sac.

This cul-de-sac begins already in *The Divided Self* which posited two distinct realms – the true self and the false self system. Nevertheless, this need not lead to the conclusions that Laing reached. Winnicott, another exponent of the true self/false self view, solved the problem differently. Basically, he did not persist with the distinction but instead presented the concept of the 'third area', the space of playing, which escapes the inside/outside dialectic. This enabled Winnicott to formulate some of the most original thinking within the psycho-analytical idiom.[9]

But Laing pushed his duality right to the limit without ever really finding a way out of it. At the time Laing was in the limelight there were not many who noticed this inconsistency;[10] most of all, Laing's views on madness and oppression were taken at his rhetorical level. To some he was a prophet, to others he was becoming dangerously irresponsible.

Finally, it may well be that it was *The Bird of Paradise*, which Laing added at the end of *The Politics of Experience* volume, that tipped the scale. Strictly speaking, it has nothing to do with psychiatry. It is a purely literary piece, a poetic stream of consciousness, intercepted with grisly images from medical training, from his native Glasgow, and some Eastern imagery. It does not seek to prove a point, it is not an essay with a line of argument. As with any writing of this type it does not appeal to reason but to an aesthetic sensitivity. But for many it was simply too much. The closing sentence, 'If I could turn you on, if I could drive you out of your wretched mind, if I could tell you I would let you know' (PE:156), was regarded, for some reason, as proof that Laing was out of his mind. Some thought that the whole piece was induced by LSD, some thought of it as evidence that Laing himself had finally gone mad. Had this been written by a regular writer and had it been published in some regular literary anthology no-one would have batted an eyelid. But coming from a psychiatrist . . .? Maybe Artaud was, after all, right.

NOTES

1 The one breakthrough in establishing an organic cause for a mental disease goes back to the nineteenth century, when some forms of insanity were linked with syphilis. This gave psychiatrists the hope of advancing further the organic model of illness but no other comparable discoveries have since been made.

2 Laing did, however, quote a passage from Artaud's 'Van Gogh, The Man Suicided by Society' in his last book *Wisdom, Madness and Folly* (WMF:13).

3 The best-known accounts are Coate (1964) and Bateson (ed. 1974) as well as an excellent collection of accounts of a psychotic experience in Kaplan (ed. 1964).

4 I can only think of one commentary which points this out, i.e. Britton (1974).

5 The works in question are *Psychiatry and Anti-Psychiatry* (1967) and *The Language of Madness* (1980), amongst others.

6 See for example Jacoby (1975) where Laing and Cooper are treated as indistinguishable.

7 After the double bind Bateson went on to formulate a sort of cybernetics of the self. In this view the self is a system of interaction which follows the cybernetical model. It happens that such a system is fundamentally flawed, calling for some corrective experiences, of which psychosis could be one. Probably the clearest statement of this position is Bateson's paper discussing the work of Alcoholics Anonymous (Bateson 1973: 280–308).

8 Bateson had worked in New Guinea and Bali with Malinowski and Radcliffe-Brown, the two outstanding anthropologists of his time. In fact,

Bateson had his first inkling of the double bind after observing the Balinese society.

9 Winnicott's false self/true self concept was developed in 'Ego Distortion in Terms of True–False Self' (Winnicott 1960), the concept of playing comes in his *Playing and Reality* (Winnicott 1982). For a more extensive discussion of this problem see Kotowicz (1993).

10 Two commentators who addressed themselves to this problem were Sedgwick (1972) and Jacoby (1975).

Chapter 5

Psychiatry and freedom

I

Behind the theoretician who drew existential descriptions of psychotics, analysed and theorized on family communication and spoke of the transcendental element in the psychotic breakdown there was also Laing the doctor, psychiatrist and psychoanalyst. Laing had a strong intellectual drive but he was not an armchair psychiatrist, his writings were very much grounded in his clinical experience. He went through medical training and during his first few years in psychiatric hospitals Laing dealt with people in the most appalling conditions imaginable. He was broken into his profession just like anyone else and he emerged from it with the simple conviction that patients had to be treated as human beings. This would seem an obvious thing but perhaps it is not so obvious if we remember that mainstream psychiatry is based on a contrary conviction, namely, that between madness and sanity there lies an unbridgeable abyss. This Laing never tired to point out, and this is why Harry Stack Sullivan's statement that 'we are all much more simply human than otherwise, be we happy and successful, contented and detached, miserable or mentally disordered, or whatever' (Sullivan 1953:16), has been so often quoted as a revelatory insight.

In the early days, when Laing was employed in a mental hospital, his distinctly different approach was already evident. Laing was put to work in a female refractory ward filled with chronic cases. 'Most of them had been in hospital for years. Most of them had electric shocks and insulin to no avail. Several had lobotomies. This was the end of the line' (WMF:114). The ward was the usual bedlam. It was tense, the nurses were constantly harassed, the dishevelled patients wandered aimlessly around. Together with two other psychiatrists Laing decided to carry out an experiment. They arranged to have a separate room. It was large, bright and it had no beds. Eleven women were chosen to spend their days in this room instead of on the ward. There they could knit, sew, read, engage in some other pastimes or simply do nothing. Two nurses were assigned to them and their sole task was to spend as much time as possible in the room with the eleven women; they were not required to participate in the life of the rest of the ward. The changes came quickly and were very marked. The tension decreased within a week. The patients were 'better behaved', the nurses did not feel harassed. As time went on the situation kept improving. Cooking facilities were installed, the patients and nurses started forming personal rapports. With the help of the nurses Laing kept a record of the changes and together with the two other psychiatrists involved in the project, Cameron and McGhie, he published in *The Lancet* in 1955 a report on the experiment, 'Patient and Nurse Effects of Environmental Changes in the Care of Chronic Schizophrenics'. A few lines from this paper show some of the concerns which are typical of Laing's later writings.

> [We] started this work with the idea of giving patients and nurses opportunity to develop interpersonal relationships of reasonably enduring nature . . . Our experience has shown, we think, that the barrier between patients and staff is not erected solely by the patients, but is a mutual construction. The removal of this barrier is a mutual activity.

> (Laing, Cameron, McGhie 1955:1384)

The results were really encouraging: the condition of the women improved so much that after a year all eleven were discharged.

And then came a thought-provoking sequel. Something was also going on outside the hospital – within eighteen months all eleven women were back inside.

Laing recounted this experience on two further occasions, first in *The Facts of Life* and the second time in the autobiographical *Wisdom, Madness and Folly.*[1] In the latter Laing recounts another interesting story from his early days as a psychiatrist. This one comes from the time of Laing's third appointment in the psychiatric unit of the Glasgow University Department of Psychiatry and it is the last case that Laing published. Written lightly and poignantly, it is as good as any of the other cases he had presented. It is a story of a fourteen-year-old boy who one day returned home and found his mother dead. She had tuberculosis and had died choking on her own vomit and blood. Thereafter his father never stopped telling him that it was his birth that brought about his mother's illness. Then one day, two months later, coming back home, the boy found his father hanging in the living-room. Soon he became a gibbering wreck and ended in hospital. He presented a truly obnoxious state. He was smelly, dirty, he hallucinated, he was incontinent. As he stumbled around the ward he effortlessly antagonized everyone in sight, so he was disliked and shunned. His prognosis was poor and he was considered for the long-stay ward which meant a more or less guaranteed career as a chronic schizophrenic. During the boy's several-week period at the ward Laing spent at least an hour a day talking to him. He felt that, although in a really wretched state, the boy stood a chance. The only option Laing could think of, other than the long-stay ward, was to take him home, to join him, his wife and their three children, all under the age of four. It proved a resounding success. The boy improved so rapidly that after three months a foster family was arranged for him and he never went back to hospital. Laing had a very precise idea as to what contributed to the boy's dramatic improvement.

> It was glaringly obvious to me that the success of the venture all hinged on his relation to Anne [Laing's wife]. She is one of the least emotionally hypocritical people I have ever met and has very little patience with it in others. She gave him very little to go crazy about on that score and she did not let him get away with that sort of thing on his part. So they got on very well.
>
> (WMF:142)

As simple as that. But there is much more to this story, there is also the credit that Laing himself deserves. Obviously before taking the boy home he had to establish a good rapport with him. In fact Laing describes the conversations they had at the hospital ward. The boy had quite a fantastic system of references. He believed that cosmic rays affected him, he was part of a world-wide network of people with some mysterious mission, the hospital ward was a sort of spherical spaceship he happened to be in. What the actual stories the boy had to tell were is not very important here; what matters, however, is that they show Laing's effortless facility to engage in the barmiest of conversations. This facility was part of his clinical strength: he had no trouble whatsoever in meeting a psychotic on his/her territory. There is an amusing story that really brings this home.

During one of his visits to the States Laing was taken to a psychiatric ward. He was shown to a room where there was a girl, sitting naked on the floor and rocking. She had not spoken to anyone for months. The staff wanted to see how Laing, the great guru of schizophrenics, would handle this case. Laing went into the room, stripped off naked, sat next to the girl and started rocking together with her. Within twenty minutes they were chatting. When he came out he expressed surprise that it had not occurred to anyone to do the same.[2]

These case descriptions, as many others, suggest that Laing had a real clinical and therapeutic gift. But he did not write anything which much elucidates the practice of therapy. Laing follows the mould of classical psychiatric literature, in the sense that almost all the case studies that he presents concentrate on the description of a condition, albeit in existential or communicational terms, but say nothing about the therapeutic process. After coming to London from Glasgow Laing went through the rigours of training as a psychoanalyst at the Institute of Psycho-Analysis. This shows in his ample usage of psychoanalytical language although it seems that it did not inform the way he worked very much. Laing had a private practice but the impression one has is that he did not have the temperament for the long, week in, week out grind of analytical work, although he did that too. He seems to have preferred to rely on his intuition to try to cut through the knots rather than painstakingly try to untie them. There is one extremely interesting example of what cutting through a knot may mean. It does not come from anything Laing wrote but from a film of a Laing workshop.[3]

A young woman is relating to him a problem that is haunting her. When she was six or seven she was abused sexually by her father. But she cannot remember whether her father had intercourse with her or not. Sometimes she thinks he only sexually played with her, sometimes she feels he went all the way. The memory is too elusive and however much she tries to remember the incident she does not succeed in making it any clearer. She is stuck with not being able to remember; that is her problem. After listening to her story Laing answers: 'Your future does not depend on that', and he goes on to tell her that only if she realizes that, only then, will she be free to remember the incident instead of being haunted by it.

There is something magic in this simple reply. It cuts right through the vicious circle the woman is in. Laing redefines the problem. Rather than joining the woman in her desperate attempts to remember the details of the event, Laing first attempts to untie her from it. He asks her to abandon a belief, probably never questioned before, that all that follows in her life depends on her ability to recall the incident precisely.

It is important to underline that he is not telling her to forget it, nothing of the sort. If she realizes that she can be free from it then she will also be free to remember it. She has to step outside the frame in which she enclosed her problem. (We have no way of knowing what the woman in question made of Laing's response. On the film she gives the impression of being quite startled, as though this one obvious thought had never occurred to her; but this is of course only an impression.)

II

From such few vignettes we can glean something about the way Laing sometimes was with his patients. Laing's own accounts[4] and the anecdotes that float around show him as unorthodox in his approach, to say the least. About the only thing that resembled the usual procedure was that he made appointments and saw people in his consulting room. (Even this was not necessarily a hard and fast rule as he was also known to go for walks to the park with his patients.) Otherwise anything could happen. For instance, for some years he experimented with LSD in his consulting room.[5] But Laing did not write anything about his therapeutic practice, and unlike many others from his profession he did not seek to build his reputation around case studies. Yet one case is always linked with his name – Mary Barnes – and with her Laing's most ambitious project, the community of Kingsley Hall.

Kingsley Hall was Laing's attempt to bring together theoretical convictions and practice. It was to be an asylum for those who would normally end up in psychiatric hospitals, a place where they would be able to live through their psychosis without the interference of psychiatric intervention. The idea was not entirely new. Maxwell Jones had already been running for some time a therapeutic community at Mill Hill Hospital and David Cooper had just started an experimental psychiatric ward, Villa 21, at Shenley Hospital.

These were projects run within psychiatric hospitals. Kingsley Hall was from the outset conceived as completely independent from any medical hierarchy. Laing created with several colleagues a charitable body, The Philadelphia Association, to give the new community legal grounding. Free from the rules of the medical profession, Laing and his colleagues could set up the project according to their own vision. In their community they would attempt to create an environment in which the traditional roles of staff and patient would not be played out. Although medically trained people were the driving force behind the project no such qualification would be required of anyone who wanted to join the community as a helper. All the members of the community would live together in the same place without any distinction of role. It was not to be a treatment centre but a place of welcome for those in distress.

It took time before a suitable building was found. After a year's search a five-year lease was arranged on a large house in East London. It could accommodate fourteen people. Soon afterwards most of the members of the newly formed association moved in and before long the place filled up with 'patients'. Mary Barnes was amongst the first to move in and she became the community's most celebrated resident. Together with her therapist Joseph Berke she wrote a book, *Mary Barnes. Two Accounts of a Journey Through Madness*. She describes in the book her childhood, adolescence, first breakdowns, treatments in hospitals (electroshocks amongst others), her first meeting with Laing, the wait for more than a year for the community to be formed during which time she was in therapy with Aaron Esterson, and finally her move into the community. There she regressed into an almost infant-like state, she refused food, smeared the walls of her room with faeces, and smeared herself as well. Then, encouraged by others, she took up painting and, going through a series of 'ups and downs' (Mary Barnes's own expression), she slowly emerged out of her madness. In the parts that he wrote, Joseph Berke describes in more detail how the community operated and gives his side of the work with Mary Barnes. It all adds up to a very moving account and the celebrity of Mary Barnes's 'journey through madness' is understandable as it is quite a remarkable story.

The book is also the major source of our knowledge of Kingsley Hall. Otherwise not much has been written about it.[6] At the time the community was still active Laing wrote a paper, 'Metanoia: Some Experiences at Kingsley Hall, London', (Laing 1968) but as it was never reprinted in any of his chief publications (*The Politics of Experience* and *The Politics of the Family* were compilations of earlier articles and talks) it was little known. A few years later in *The Politics of the Family* Laing gave a two-page 'report' on the project, with some very basic dry figures and no commentary. Apart from that, nothing.

However, from the little that is known a clear enough picture emerges. Kingsley Hall was a fully independent set-up and the group who began it were fully committed to the diffusion of traditional psychiatric roles. It was not easy. Already in his very first paper from his mental hospital days in Glasgow, Laing had noted that the barrier between patients and staff is a mutual construction and that the removal of this barrier must likewise be a mutual activity. As it turned out, the sheer fact of being doctors vested Laing and the other psychiatrists with a prestige which they did not necessarily seek. Mary Barnes, for one, was very insistent that those who looked after her were 'properly trained'. For example, at one critical moment, when it was imperative that she start eating, only the intervention of Aaron Esterson, a doctor, could persuade her to begin taking food again. The stability of the whole community largely depended on the doctors and not surprisingly their word carried more weight. It also seems that there were occasions, although very rare, when someone had to be restrained, almost in the old-fashioned straitjacket style.[7]

Nevertheless, there is no doubt that the community was run on genuinely democratic lines. Power sharing and decision taking within the community were genuine group processes and the level of tolerance that existed at Kingsley Hall was quite remarkable. Mary Barnes really wreaked havoc in the place, and she was not the only one. Tolerance in the surrounding neighbourhood was less unequivocal. Local residents did not always find it easy to put up with the noise and unusual comings and goings of the community and there were periods of hostility. At times some locals would end their drinking sessions by smashing windows of the house. Relations could have probably been better but those in charge of the operation did not put any effort into working with the surrounding neighbourhood, this was not in Kingsley Hall's brief. A Laingian therapeutic community was conceived as an island, a sort of psychiatric Epicurean garden, largely indifferent to the outside world.

From the sources available we can make out how the community operated but a level-headed critical examination of the project from someone really familiar with it would be welcome – many important issues came up, not only in Mary Barnes's story, and there are things to be learnt from it.

One very important question which one would like to have addressed, at least tentatively, is some assessment of the kind of toll this level of involvement exerts. How long can a therapist reside in a community like this? Laing left after a year, Esterson did not last any longer, and the maximum any therapist stayed was two years.[8] Does it say something that the only person who stayed from the beginning to the end was Mary Barnes?

III

Mary Barnes's 'journey through madness' became a celebrated case. Her paintings were exhibited, her book was widely read. She became a much quoted example of an anti-psychiatric 'cure', as the term 'anti-psychiatry' was beginning to gain currency just as her book came out.

The actual term was coined by David Cooper in his book *Psychiatry and Anti-Psychiatry*. The terrain that Cooper traversed in his book was much the same as the one we find in Laing's works. Psychiatry is founded on violence, the hierarchical structure of a mental hospital is a structure of power; 'schizophrenia' is not a scientifically established fact but a set of prejudices, it is a 'microsocial' crisis which usually begins in the family; those labelled 'schizophrenic' need help which is radically different from what is offered in the traditional institution. In Cooper's view, the psychiatrist should be more like a shaman, a guide who can lead out of the crisis. In essence Cooper's position is almost identical to Laing's – *Psychiatry and Anti-Psychiatry* is the work in which Cooper is closest to Laing – only sometimes the tone is, if anything, more trenchant. What sets the book apart is Cooper's description of the experimental ward at Shenley Hospital, Villa 21, which he led for four years.[9]

Villa 21 was a ward for young men between the ages of fifteen and twenty. Cooper thought that an alternative approach could be most effective with people who were at the beginning of their psychiatric career. The majority of them had already had been diagnosed as schizophrenic, the others as suffering from affective disorders. The staff, drawn from the traditional set – nurses, occupational therapists, doctors – were carefully selected and to begin with the ward was run like a structured therapeutic community. Daily community meetings, therapeutic groups, workshops, staff meetings were the principal activities on the ward. The staff began with quite clearly defined roles but the aim was to loosen these structures as the time went on. As could be expected, the diffusion of roles was not a straightforward affair. One problem which was evident right from the beginning was the problem of the authority of the doctor. It turned out to be so deeply ingrained in this institution as to be virtually impossible to eradicate. Still, the venture, while it lasted, was a modest success and many interesting lessons were learnt. But Cooper concluded that any future work of this kind had to be done outside the great institutions (Cooper 1967).

IV

The anti-psychiatric movement[10] was not confined to Britain. In other countries opposition to the psychiatric idiom was also growing and alternative projects were set up. Their beginnings were different and their aims not quite the same but they all belonged to a shared platform of a fight against the institution, against the psychiatric diagnosis and for the restoration of legal, moral and human rights to those who were invalidated by the psychiatric machinery. One occasion during which these issues became prominent was during an extraordinary eruption which took place in 1970 at the psychiatric clinic of the University of Heidelberg, West Germany.

The Heidelberg University clinic was not a regular psychiatric set-up. Being attached to the university it served as a training ground for those who were expected to get far in the profession. The patients were not of the run-of-the-mill mental hospital type either; they were young, educated, often students. The build-up to the events was not unusual. It began when the director of the clinic decided to introduce new methods of work. Psychotherapy groups were introduced, a group for old people from outside the clinic was run. The project ran into difficulties with the university authorities and after about a year the clinic's director, Spazier, resigned. His replacement, Kretz, was appointed to restore the clinic's old ways. One of Spazier's assistants, Wolfgang Huber, wanted to continue with the innovations. After about a year of disagreements Huber was dismissed from his post.

One unusual factor in these otherwise unremarkable developments was the way the disagreements were couched. Huber did not argue from the clinical point of view; that is, it was not that he attempted to convince others that his methods were better. Instead, his argument was political. He wanted changes in the clinic so it would serve the interests of the patients rather the interests of the staff. That he had a point was vindicated by the official reason given for his dismissal from his post – he refused to attend academic conferences, insisting that his time was better spent on the ward with his patients. But whatever the arguments the affair seemed to be heading towards a typical end: the rebelling doctor was removed from his post and everything was expected to return to normal.

But this is not what happened. Clearly Huber's work with the patients left a deep mark because as the news of his dismissal reached the clinic they convened a general assembly. (This, they claimed in their document, was the first genuine patients' assembly in the history of psychiatry.)

Claiming the patient's right to treatment and the right to choose their doctor the assembly demanded the restoration of Huber and dismissal of the clinic's director. The reply was to remove around sixty of the patients from the clinic. At this point the Socialist Patients' Collective (Sozialistisches Patienten Kollektiv, SPK) was formed. The patients went on a hunger strike and this extracted a promise from the university authorities to the effect that other premises would be provided for them where they could continue their treatment with Huber. The agreement was sabotaged from the very beginning. The premises were not ready, Huber's prescriptions were not accepted in the Heidelberg pharmacies. After four months of uncertainties the patients occupied the offices of the university Rectorate and their programme hardened. Now they demanded control of the monies, control of the clinic, a separate building. They also demanded full recognition as a university body. The university authorities appointed three experts with the view of examining the status of SPK within the institution but by then things had gone too far; it was no longer an affair confined to the university.

One would have to be an expert on German politics to disentangle all the complexities of the developments. The university, the local government, the Ministry of Education were involved, and finally the law stepped in. After a massive operation of a type usually reserved for dangerous terrorists (both ends of the street closed off, dogs, etc.), the police evicted the patients from their premises. Several patients were arrested as well as Huber and some of his associates. The story of SPK lasted little more than a year. All that remained was for the law to dispense its justice. Several people were sent to prison. Wolfgang Huber was sentenced to four and a half years of prison, the maximum possible for the 'head of a criminal association'. His wife Ursula was sentenced to four years. Huber served the sentence in full, including twenty months in isolation. Others went on the run and spent some years abroad under assumed names.

This extraordinary turn of events has to be seen in the context of the then political mood of Germany. It was the time when the student protest was transforming into harder forms of opposition – the Baader–Meinhof group was beginning to operate and the authorities were responding with a comprehensive crackdown on all left-wing groups. Suspected members of these groups were banned from public employment, arrests and imprisonments were quite frequent. SPK quickly became entangled in this political game. Within a short time it transformed itself from a psychiatric pressure group into a revolutionary cell. There was a considerable campaign in the media against

SPK and the positions on both sides grew harder and n
Some contact between SPK and sympathizers of Baader–
take place. This and the rhetoric of SPK gave the autho.
pretext to act (and they did not usually need much). Documei
present the problem of psychiatry, psychiatric illness, or any il_ _ss as a
phenomenon which is nourished by the capitalist system. The
psychiatric ward is one of the places where the struggle against
capitalist oppression is concentrated as the psychiatric patient is the
embodiment of this oppression. The well-educated elite patients of the
psychiatric system turned themselves into the revolutionary vanguard
first opposing those who claimed to be helping them – the psychiatrists.
The sheer lawlessness of psychiatry burst into the open in Heidelberg.

SPK was the most radical and extreme psychiatric event from the
epoch of anti-psychiatry. Its 'clinical' value cannot be spoken of
because no project that lasts only a year, fighting throughout to survive
as a legitimate entity, can produce clinical 'results'. And even despite
this, during the arguments and at the trial of the psychiatrists, figures
were produced to refute accusations that their activities were
detrimental to the well-being of the patients. But what was really at
stake was power. SPK made no secret that it wanted to wrest power
away from the authorities. Yet its relation to power was complex
because, ironically, at the same time it also fought to be recognized as a
body rightly belonging to the university and to the very end its headed
paper read: 'Socialist Patients' Collective of the University of
Heidelberg'. It would take more than just the parent–child model to
analyse this fight against and attachment to power. But finally one
remembers most the sheer brutality with which this outbreak of
resistance was stamped out.

V

The greatest experiment in alternative psychiatry took place in Italy. Its
vision was enormous, it lasted for longer than any other and its effects
were more wide-ranging than anywhere else. Up until the 1960s the
Italian psychiatric service consisted of no more than a number of big
provincial mental hospitals run along custodial lines and a few
university clinics. Social psychiatry, therapeutic communities, and
other psychiatric innovations did not percolate through to Italy, things
had remained the same since the beginning of the century – the
legislation which governed the country's mental health services dated
from 1904.

The change began with the appointment of a young psychiatrist, Franco Basaglia, to run a provincial hospital in Gorizia, right on the Italian–Yugoslav border. Basaglia, like Laing, began his opposition to traditional psychiatry through reading the existential and phenomenological texts but his early career was different. He came from a university clinic, possibly quite similar to the one in Heidelberg, and he had no real experience of a provincial mental asylum. Together with a team of chosen people Basaglia set out to change the hospital into a humane environment. The hospital which had kept its patients locked up for decades was to become an open institution. The first stage involved the removal of all physical restraints – bars were removed from windows, wards were no longer locked, patients were allowed to keep their personal belongings. Straightforward measures of this kind allowed a rapport between the doctors and the patients to develop to the point where (as Basaglia hoped) the patients could form themselves into self-governing groups. Basaglia and his team also opened a café and a beauty parlour in the hospital grounds. These were later taken over by the patients. The use of electroshocks was suspended, medication was drastically reduced. The main activities at the hospital were endless meetings which involved all the patients who cared to attend and all the staff. Transforming a backward provincial mental hospital into an open community cannot be a simple task and many difficulties arose. The hospital had 500 patients, 150 nurses and eight doctors. Any changes in the nature of the community would have to transform the circulation of power within it. To begin with the innovations were generated almost exclusively by the new team. These were naturally directed towards the patients, many of them institutionalized by decades of residence in the hospital. The nurses, however, found their traditional roles much undermined and in the earlier phase they much resisted the new regime.

The experiment worked on the whole very well, so well, in fact, that after a few years Basaglia started getting ready for the next stage of his work. Consistently developing his ideas he came to conclude that however humane the hospital environment can be made it would still remain unsatisfactory. A comfortable hospital would perhaps please the inmates but it would still remain a hospital with the ideology of degradation and exclusion imprinted in it. The hospital embodies the basic contradiction that is at the root of psychiatry – the contradiction between *cura* (therapy, treatment) and *custodia* (custody, guardianship). The only solution was to aim to dismantle the institution altogether. To carry out this kind of project Basaglia needed the full co-operation of the local authorities as it would involve the community at large. He did not find this in Gorizia and in 1969, after eight years, Basaglia left.

Before leaving Basaglia took care to document the project and the book of the experience, *The Institution Negated* (*L'Istituzione Negata*), published in 1968, became one of the key texts of the Italian left, giving Gorizia the status of celebrity and nourishing further experimentation. About half a dozen different projects followed, some of them run by members of the first Gorizia team.

In 1971 an opportunity to push further the de-institutionalization of psychiatric services presented itself. Basaglia was invited to reorganize the entire local mental health services of Trieste, a town of 300,000 inhabitants. The job description could have not suited Basaglia better as the service available that he was meant to reorganize consisted of one huge mental hospital and nothing else. Basaglia brought with him a team of like-minded psychiatrists, psychologists and others, and set to work. The aim, right from the beginning, was to lead to the dissolution of the hospital and the transference of the services into the community. However, it was not simply a case of deciding to shut down the hospital and to set up alternative services down the road. It was to be a long process at the end of which the community's resources and level of awareness would be such that the hospital would become obsolete. Work had to be done in the hospital while it lasted and a great deal of work within the community was necessary as well. In the first part of the task the team could largely draw on the Gorizia experience. Community teams were set up and various activities were organized to break the wall between the population and the hospital inmates.

> Important films and plays were put on [in the hospital], which were open to the public and often attracted a large audience from outside the hospital. Theatre groups and painters also contributed to the activities: one project involved building a large blue papier-mâché horse – 'Marco the Horse' – as a kind of mascot, which was then wheeled through the town in procession to the accompaniment of dramatic performances. Holidays were also organized for groups of patients, staying at seaside resorts in regular hotels. Thus, it was not enough simply to remove the *physical* barriers between patients and the outside world: activities had to be devised to break down the *social* barriers which still remained.
>
> (Basaglia 1981:188)

The achievements in Trieste were tremendous. Seven years after the experiment began the hospital was officially closed. In its place there was a network of mental health centres and crises were dealt with by a small emergency unit, attached to the general hospital, which was staffed by the psychiatrists. The experiment attracted enormous interest and was studied by the World Health Organization as a possible recommended model to be applied on a wider scale. In Italy the prominence of these experiments made the issue of the laws governing the provision of care for the mentally ill enter the political agenda. In 1978 the parliament voted in a new law, the equivalent of a Mental Health Act, which turned the old 1904 legislation inside out. It declared the need to dismantle hospitals; it restored full civic rights to those diagnosed mentally ill; it dropped all references to the 'dangerousness' of the mentally ill and in general took away from psychiatry the right to detain or treat anyone against their will. The psychiatric system was to cease to act as society's protector against the mentally ill. The law was not exactly how Basaglia and his colleagues would want it, there were misgivings about some of the details,[11] but it was a great success, and the aim to dismantle the old system had been largely achieved. The psychiatrists won the political argument and the new law was popularly called 'Basaglia's law'.

The implementation of the law was less comprehensive than was hoped for. The volatile political climate, the economic situation and many other factors did not make it possible to translate the Trieste model nationwide with anything like the same success. But this is another story.[12]

VI

One of the distinctive features of the Italian scene was the number of people – mostly, but not exclusively, psychiatrists – involved. So while we have referred to Basaglia there was in fact a team working together. Many of the collaborators distinguished themselves in other projects and together with Basaglia the names of Franca Ongaro Basaglia, Agostino Pirella, Giovanni Jervis, Antonio Slavich must be mentioned. The number of psychiatrists that supported these new developments was large enough to merit the setting up of an official movement called Democratic Psychiatry. Without the involvement of a considerable number of people the effects of these experiments could not have had such wide-ranging political implications. The two influential works that appeared, *The Institution Negated* and *What is Psychiatry?* (*Che cos'è la Psichiatria?*), were collected efforts put together under the editorship of Basaglia and were in effect the programme of Democratic Psychiatry.

Basaglia and his colleagues shared many convictions with other anti-psychiatrists. Like Laing, Basaglia realized very early on that the approach in standard textbooks only estranges the psychiatrist from the patient. Also like Laing, Basaglia first came across ideas different from the medically oriented texts in the writings of existential and phenomenological psychiatrists. But whatever attraction existential analyses held for Basaglia in his early days they are not present in his work in Gorizia and Trieste. It was the political agenda that drove his project along. Basaglia never concentrated on what constitutes the nature of madness; throughout his career his attention was focused on society's response to madness. He was particularly sensitive to the question of the patients' legal rights. Characteristically, when the Trieste hospital closed down Basaglia did not make any claims about having 'cured' the mentally ill of the town; he was well aware that there remained people who needed help. His achievement, he would say, lay in his having played a part in liberating the patients from the oppression of the psychiatric institutions.

The writings of Basaglia and his collaborators give us a clear survey of the different influences behind their programme. They knew very well the works of the American sociologists and they were very impressed with Goffman's *Asylums*, to which they refer frequently. There is also something of Foucault's confrontation with unreason in Basaglia's claim that by liberating the mad from the asylums the ordinary citizen is confronted with the madness that is in society.

> It must be emphasized, in case any confusion on this point still remains, that what is proposed here is not mere *tolerance* of mental illness, as the alternative to suppression. When the mentally ill are no longer segregated – conceptually as well as spatially – we are forced to recognize their peculiarities and at the same time discover our own: for 'normality' can be just as much a distortion as madness. Only if relationships with the 'sick' person are maintained unbroken can his fellows continue to recognize him as one of them, and to identify their own needs with his.
>
> (Basaglia 1981:192)

As far as the actual practice was concerned *Psichiatria Democratica* drew many lessons from various experiments that had taken place in England. John Conolly, the nineteenth-century psychiatrist who instituted in the Hanwell Asylum a regime without physical and medical restraint, was one of the ideological godfathers of Democratic Psychiatry. The Italians studied Maxwell Jones's therapeutic community project and they knew Laing and visited Kingsley Hall. Interestingly, they put Kingsley Hall in the tradition of community care going back to Conolly. Their own thinking was far more politically oriented. In many respects their arguments were similar to those of SPK – the mentally ill are part of the illness of the capitalist society, liberating them is a political act. In fact, it is impressive how consistent the members of Democratic Psychiatry were in their ideological stance, always arguing their position on political grounds. Their rhetoric was unmistakably from the radical left. It is symptomatic that the question of 'cost-effectiveness' never played a role in the arguments, though on the ground they proved quite deft in solving economic problems.

VII

SPK, Democratic Psychiatry and Kingsley Hall all belong in the universe of anti-psychiatry and yet they are radically different, or to put it in another way, they reflect different aspects of the movement to reform psychiatry.

The differences had no doubt something to do with the personalities of the principal protagonists, Huber, Basaglia and Laing. But it is interesting to see that they also seem to reflect the political conditions in their respective countries. The events around SPK were very characteristic of the political climate in Germany at the time. Democratic Psychiatry was part of the Italian left, and reflected the strength of the Communist Party who had a great following in the country and great popular support. Nowhere did psychiatry gain such high profile as in Italy. Kingsley Hall operated very much within the English tradition – The Philadelphia Association, the official organization behind the community, based its independence on its charitable organization status. The outcome of these experiments also followed a course which in hindsight seems almost inevitable. In Germany it was violent confrontation; in Italy, due to the strength of the Communist party, there were far-reaching changes; in England the therapeutic community projects suffered the marginalization that charitable bodies invariably do.[13] This dimension of the experiments cannot be overlooked as psychiatry is a political problem *par excellence* and, at least to an extent, the success or failure has to be judged on political grounds. The Italians were aware right from the beginning that Kingsley Hall, as a private community, showed its indifference to and misunderstanding of the wider political aspects of psychiatric work. But although the Italians worked along entirely different lines, Kingsley

Hall-type communities would do very well in a psychiatric landscape as envisaged by Basaglia and his colleagues.

SPK revealed the political dimension that went with the new thinking and the level of opposition that existed. Democratic Psychiatry showed the extent to which the social changes are possible. And what do we learn from the experience of Kingsley Hall? In comparison with the Italian achievements it pales into insignificance.[14] But there is something special about it, although it has to be viewed on the 'small is beautiful' scale. What marks out Kingsley Hall is that it was conceived as a project where the madwoman and madman could be met on their terrain, where some form of genuine dialogue with Unreason could happen. Perhaps this was the only project where such a thing could really take place, even if only sporadically. The book about Kingsley Hall is the one book we should regret Laing never wrote.

Kingsley Hall ended when the lease on the building ran out. Other places were set up to continue this tradition. Laing himself needed a break; during the preceding ten years he had been on the sharp edge of all these activities. As the community was winding down he was preparing to go away to Ceylon (now Sri Lanka) and India for a year. As it turned out Laing's departure brought his career as a theoretician and militant of radical psychiatry to an end.

NOTES

1 In *The Facts of Life* Laing recounts this experiment referring to twelve, rather than eleven, patients, which seems a slip.

2 This story is recounted in *R.D.Laing. A Biography* by his son Adrian C. Laing (Laing 1994:171–172).

3 This comes in a film made in 1989 by Third Mind Productions Inc., Vancouver, Canada, *Did You Used to Be R.D. Laing?*, which was shown on Channel 4 a few months after Laing's death.

4 See Mullan (1995:315–334).

5 For anyone who finds this a shocking idea it is worth remembering that there was a period when psychiatrists quite seriously explored the possibilities of using LSD in a therapeutic context. And, of course, it was then legal.

6 There is also a fictionalized account by Clancy Sigal in his *Zone of the Interior* (Sigal 1976). The book is a portrait of Laing and of life at Kingsley Hall. It is so savage (and at times hysterically funny) that it has to be taken with a pinch of salt. Interestingly, no British publisher would touch it for fear of libel action, which suggests that the book's contents have to be treated with circumspection.

7 On one occasion a particularly perturbing individual was put into a sack and tied to the bottom of the stairs, an incident Giovanni Jervis says Laing had recounted to him personally (Jervis 1977:32).

8 This was perhaps also due to it being a house in a city. In another Philadelphia Association community, a farmhouse with grounds in Oxfordshire, some therapists, together with their families, stayed longer.

9 Laing was to some extent involved in the Villa 21 project. Together with Esterson and Cooper he carried out a family therapy study there. It was published as 'Results of a Family-Orientated Therapy with Hospitalized Schizophrenics' in *British Medical Journal*, 18 December 1965.

10 Although the term 'anti-psychiatry' was rejected by many, there were nevertheless attempts to bring together the different radical practitioners into some kind of loose forum. A few congresses of anti-psychiatry were held in the mid-1970s in Paris, Brussels, Milan.

11 The one aspect that particularly worried Basaglia and his colleagues was the establishment of small psychiatric units for severe cases in general hospitals. They found it preferable to separate psychiatric hospitals but were not pleased to see the medical wedge inserted at the difficult end of psychiatry.

12 A comprehensive account of the Italian experiment can be found in Michael Donnelly's *The Politics of Mental Health in Italy* (Donnelly 1992).

13 Although during long periods such organizations could do pretty much what they pleased, they had no impact on the 'system'. The best that such a body could, and can, aspire to is to become a pressure group.

14 However, Giovanni Jervis, one of the chief architects of the Italian Democratic Psychiatry noted that:

> almost ten years after the explosion of May [1968], the situation concerning the Italian public psychiatric assistance is not brilliant: on the one hand the 'advanced' experiences are not really numerous, and perhaps they have not produced nothing really new in comparison with the better British experiences of the last fifteen or twenty years.
>
> (Jervis 1977:30)

When Jervis is referring to the British experiences he is not only referring to Kingsley Hall and Villa 21 but also to the psychotherapeutic community of Maxwell Jones. The Italians, it should be remembered, were impressed by the British tradition which goes back to John Conolly's non-restraint work in Hanwell Asylum. It should also be noted that Jervis wrote this before the 1978 parliament act was voted in, when the 1904 legislation was still the formal grounding for the psychiatrists' work.

Chapter 6

Response and legacy

I

Laing's reputation was outrageous. His views circulated widely and were taken up at every possible level. He was quoted as a contemporary sage, a seer for modern times, as the chief spokesperson of the new alternative culture which would see the demise of the capitalist system and usher in a community of heightened consciousness.[1] Much was expected of Laing. His public lectures, both in England and abroad, mostly in the US, brought in audiences of a kind that only celebrities manage to attract.[2]

Around the height of his fame many new therapies such as Gestalt, Encounter groups, transactional analysis, and Primal Scream were becoming fashionable and for a moment Laing was seen by some as in the same circuit. But this association was altogether superficial and it did not last long. Laing himself never sought to belong in this company and to anyone who took the trouble to read him carefully it was plain that he did not belong in there. Their subsequent fortunes were also different. The new American therapies of 'I'm OK, you're OK', or 'becoming a person', became commodities that could be sold to corporate business and other functionaries of the system. Laing's ideas did not lend themselves to such commercialization.

Laing's status was also recognized in some 'official' quarters. In 1973 a book about him (Friedenberg 1973) was included in the 'Modern Masters' series. Two more book-length commentaries (Collier 1977 and Howarth-Williams 1977) followed. A collection of essays on the work of Laing appeared (Boyers and Orrill 1972) as well as other commentaries. They were part of the wide response to Laing and the intensity of it, the way it was conducted, was extraordinary. Of the book-length commentaries Collier and Howarth-Williams are very helpful in disentangling the difficult aspects of Laing's work, particularly the influence of Sartre. Friedenberg is really too short and sketchy to be of much use. But we shall focus here on responses which came from commentators who held openly partisan positions. Many of them were extremely critical of Laing and some of them came from those who would be considered, at least in the popular perceptions, as of basically similar outlook, or sympathetic to Laing's work. One such example was an attack that Thomas Szasz unleashed.

II

In most of the general accounts on anti-psychiatry Szasz's work is cited as important to the thinking of the new alternative approaches and consequently he was often viewed as one from the camp. Attentive readers would have been aware of the considerable differences between Szasz and Laing but many were not. Szasz personally took care to spell out his disagreements with Laing. In 1976 in *The New Review* he published an article, 'Anti-Psychiatry: The Paradigm of a Plundered Mind'. The position from which Szasz views Laing is overtly political and the article is more an acrimonious attack than a considered critique. Szasz agrees that on some points, especially in the critique of the psychiatric system, his and Laing's views coincide. But he goes on to add that this amounts to no more than sharing the same enemy; he feels as close to Laing as Churchill did to Stalin. This turned out to be more than just a throwaway example as from the remainder of what Szasz had to say it is clear that he considered himself to be the Churchill and Laing the Stalin:

> the anti-psychiatrists are all self-declared socialists, Communists, or at least anti-capitalists and collectivists. As the Communists seek to raise the poor above the rich, so the anti-psychiatrists seek to raise the 'insane' above the 'sane'.
>
> (Szasz 1976:2)

As we can see, the sweep of those whom Szasz condemns is wide and the argument plainly crude, nothing more than a relentless anti-Communist invective which runs throughout the exposition. The residents of Kingsley Hall are referred to as 'communards' (ibid.:8), and Laing is 'a preacher of and for the "soft" underbelly of the New Left' (ibid.:4). Most of the quotes that offended Szasz's anti-Communist sentiments come from Cooper who indeed sprinkled his writings with a fair deal of 'Molotov Cocktail' imagery but in the main it makes little difference – Szasz's attack applies as much to Laing (and all other anti-psychiatrists, for that matter) as Szasz vehemently denounces all shades of critique against capitalism. This comment is characteristic of the tone and the level of argument.

> The anti-psychiatrists' view here also mirrors faithfully the envious fulminations of modern Marxists and Communists who attribute poverty of 'underdeveloped' peoples to their being robbed, mainly by Americans, of their wealth. The Chileans would be all rich if American companies did not plunder their copper mines. In this anti-capitalist, anti-colonialist perspective, riches flow from natural resources without human intervention. Such intervention only confiscates and corrupts. The Chilean sitting on top of a mountain of unmined copper is 'rich'. The child left alone with his uncorrupted self is 'sane'. Each becomes a 'victim' through plunder.
>
> (ibid.:11)

There is something quite shocking in this example of Chile – it comes not long after the CIA-backed coup deposed and killed the democratically elected left-wing president Salvadore Allende and installed the dictatorship of General Pinochet. (The nationalization of the American owned copper industry was one of the events which provoked the CIA intervention in Chilean affairs.) Shocking, but consistent with the overall tone. Szasz despises the left because it appeals to the youth of our age who 'having nothing to live for, are envious of all those who do, and want to destroy the institutions that give meaning to the lives of "normal" people' (ibid.:12). Who these 'normal' people are is not clearly spelt out but perhaps they are those who follow

> the simplest and most ancient of human truths, namely, that life is an arduous and tragic struggle; that what we call 'sanity' – what we mean by 'not being schizophrenic' – has a great deal to do with competence, earned by struggling for excellence; with compassion, hard won by confronting conflict; and with modesty and patience, acquired through silence and suffering.
>
> (ibid.:12)

This joyless Darwinian reality does not even bear contemplating.

Another part of Szasz's attack concerns Mary Barnes – 'Laing's Wolf-woman', as Szasz puts it, in an allusion to Freud's famous 'Wolfman' case. This, according to Szasz, is the same game as that of classical psychiatry because Laing, just as much as those that he opposes, remains obsessed with 'schizophrenia'.

[That] Laing's actual position on schizophrenia is quite close not only to Bleuler's but also to Freud's is strongly supported by Laing's 'Wolf-woman' – Mary Barnes. Consider the parallels. As Freud had a famous patient psychoanalyzed on the couch, so Laing has one guided through madness at Kingsley Hall. As the Wolfman had a 'neurosis', which is the sacred symbol of psychoanalysis – so Mary Barnes had a 'psychosis' which is the sacred symbol of psychiatry and anti-psychiatry. And, finally, as Freud's famous patient and the legends about him and other patients authenticated Freud as an exceptional healer of neurotics – so Laing's famous patient and the legends about her and other patients authenticate Laing as an exceptional healer of psychotics.

(ibid.:9)

We know from primary sources, namely from Mary Barnes's book, that she was Joseph Berke's, not Laing's, patient but this does not distract Szasz from his argument. It comes across the more persuasively for being linked into a chain of similar phenomena – Freud and Wolfman, Laing and Mary Barnes. But even if it were pointed out to Szasz that Mary Barnes was not Laing's patient, he would maintain his argument. He would still hold Laing to account because Laing was the prime protagonist of Kingsley Hall and he was responsible for the 'cult of authenticity', which Szasz detests. At any rate, Szasz maintains that the radicality of the case of Mary Barnes is fake. The only difference between a 'voyage' through madness and 'treatment' in a hospital is that 'in the lunatic asylum the guiding metaphors are medical, whereas in the Laingian they are Alpinistic'[?!] (ibid.:10).

Worst of all, Kingsley Hall is supported by the taxpayer as many of the residents extract 'by force or fraud' funds from the Welfare State. And so 'while Laing's tongue lashes British taxpayers for funding a society that drives people mad, his hands are picking the taxpayers' pockets' (ibid.:3). And in another colourful analogy Szasz goes on to say that 'The British taxpayer has no more of a direct vote on whether or not he wants his hard-earned money spent that way than did the American taxpayer have on paying for the war in Vietnam' (ibid.:3).

For those who associated Szasz with the critique of the psychiatric system this rampant attack must have come as a shock. But a more careful reading of Szasz's writings shows that his hostility to Laing was altogether consistent with the views he had been expounding from the very beginning of his illustrious career.

Szasz's *The Myth of Mental Illness* and *The Manufacture of Madness*, along with several other publications, have acquired a just reputation for being among the most uncompromising in their attitude towards the existing psychiatric practices. 'Institutional psychiatry' is a system which invents the notion of a mental illness. It invents it in order to incarcerate, under a medical guise, those that the society for one reason or another does not want. At this level Szasz's work was singularly helpful. The argument was simple, to the point of being oversimplified, but it was banged in with consistency and it was meticulously documented.[3] One cannot doubt the repressive element in the institution of psychiatry after going through Szasz's writings. However, Szasz goes much further. He does not accept that the State, or any other collective organization, has any role to play in the problems of mental suffering. Szasz contends that those who are named mentally ill suffer from 'problems in living', which is an inability to act out the various roles that the society expects of us. In place of the existing 'institutional psychiatry' with its custodial approach to the mentally ill, he advocates 'contractual psychiatry'. He means by this that those suffering from 'problems in living' should be legally empowered to seek help as they see fit, without the intervention of the State.

This may seem at first sight quite a reasonable approach to the problem save that at least two points must be raised in this context. First, there are those who are not quite in a state of mind to shop around for help which they could then contract out (minors, elderly, severely psychotic). Second, Szasz's anti-State crusade is conducted from the libertarian right-wing position which is singularly hostile to the idea that in responding to those who are in need of help, the community, or the State, may be animated by 'care'. Such an attitude only fosters dependence and breeds riff-raff. 'The simplest and most ancient of human truths', to repeat Szasz's lines, is that 'life is an arduous and tragic struggle'. The rewards go to those who are competent, patient, modest, silent, and who accept suffering, There is no place in it for resentful, envious leftists, or for anyone else who does not contribute to this grim freedom of a laissez-faire society.

With this in mind Szasz's campaign to abolish mental hospitals[4] cannot be put in the same bracket as other protests against the inhumanity of the psychiatric system. He is anti-Establishment but in the name of a higher law – the law of the market. And so Szasz would want to eliminate all forms of collective response to mental illness. And there is nothing particularly new in this. As long ago as 1961, Enoch Powell, the then Minister of Health, envisaged closing all mental hospitals and setting up a community care system. This has remained the policy of the Conservative Party, although it is becoming manifest that the notion of 'community care' is no more than lip service. It is one thing to shut down hospitals and another to genuinely tackle the society's response to mental illness. This is the difference between the right-wing laissez-faire cost-saving programmes and the Italian experiment, for example.[5]

III

Laing was also attacked from the left end of the ideological spectrum. In 1971 a volume of essays *Laing and Anti-Psychiatry* was published containing an article by Peter Sedgwick, 'R.D. Laing: Self, Symptom and Society'. In the Notes on Contributors to the volume Sedgwick describes his position as a 'libertarian Marxist (International Socialist)' (Boyers and Orrill 1972:10) and indeed, all his intellectual career was consistent with this description, the standpoint from which he approaches Laing.

Sedgwick gives a fairly comprehensive overview of Laing's work. He is impressed with *The Divided Self* as, as he puts it, 'one of the most difficult philosophies [existentialism] was brought to bear on one of the most baffling of mental conditions, in a manner which, somewhat surprisingly, helped to clarify both' (Sedgwick 1972:13). Another reason for singling out Laing's first book is that there is no hint of mysticism in it, no hint of the psychotic as a prophet of a super-sensory world. Sedgwick also points out that in *The Divided Self* the condition of schizophrenia is viewed as a syndrome attributable to an individual, rather than a distorted pattern of communications, as Laing held in his later writings, and this Sedgwick thinks is correct. From then on Laing's work, as far as Sedgwick is concerned, deteriorates. Sedgwick analyses the convergence of the influence of Sartre and Bateson on Laing's theorizing with a particularly caustic presentation of the work of the researchers into the new theories of human communication. Sedgwick does not think much of Laing's views concerning the family and finds a great deal at fault with *Sanity, Madness and the Family*. His main objection is that although the aim of the book was to make the schizophrenic experience intelligible within the context of the family, Laing and Esterson did so by excluding from their presentation the actual schizophrenic symptom. This is specifically evident from the fact that no incidents of a word-salad are presented in the material, that all the exchanges are perfectly coherent. Sedgwick goes as far as to state that after reading the cases we are at a loss to know what is really the matter with these supposedly schizophrenic women. This is obviously an exaggeration.

But these criticisms were mild in comparison to what Sedgwick had to say about Laing's mystical leanings and the idea that the schizophrenic is 'engaged in a lonely voyage back towards the primeval point of oneness' (ibid.:38). To Sedgwick this is dangerous nonsense and a detraction from the serious task of addressing mental suffering.

However, these criticisms aside, Sedgwick came to conclude that Laing's mysticism did not run very deep and, despite a few other blind alleys into which his theorizing strayed, the main tendencies in Laing's work could be developed.

> The theory and the therapy of mainstream psychiatry are bound to be indebted to Laing, and to similar vanguard trends in social medicine, if only because no other rival approach, whether biochemical or environmental, seems to possess any dynamic or momentum of comparable power. Laing's theories of schizophrenia were powerfully aided, in the public view, by the distinguished cultural and philosophical apparatus in which they reposed: his popularity rode with the great timelessness of many of these supporting ideas, which often raised vital issues of a kind traditionally ignored by doctors, natural scientists and even social scientists.
>
> (ibid.:45)

And just as Sedgwick had completed his essay, Laing went off to the Orient for his sabbatical. The fact that he chose as his destination Ceylon, a country gripped by a repressive regime, shocked Sedgwick and he added a Postscript to his essay. He says, 'Withdrawal is not always a betrayal: but in this case, what else is it?' (ibid.:46) and then continues, 'whatever is progressive in the British existential-psycho-analytic school must now be taken up, developed and transcended by people with a firmer commitment and a stronger, far stronger, ideology' (ibid.:47).

Ten years later Sedgwick issued *Psycho Politics* (Sedgwick 1982). Here the analysis of Laing's work is greatly extended and put into a far wider context. In addition to Laing, Sedgwick subjects to scrutiny the influence of three other figures associated with the anti-psychiatric movement – Erving Goffman, Michel Foucault and Thomas Szasz. Each one of them comes in for heavy criticism. But before launching into his commentaries Sedgwick presents his opening premise. He points out that all the anti-psychiatric theoreticians take for granted a clear distinction between physical illness and mental illness. He contends that we can only approach any coherent understanding of mental illness if we first examine the meaning of illness in our society. He goes on to argue that once we take this position – rather than posit from the outset an *a priori* distinction between the 'objective' physical illness and 'relativist' mental illness – then we will find that the two belong in the same terrain. It has to be pointed out that Sedgwick is not seeking to bring back mental illness into the domain of medicine, or at least into medicine as it has developed in modern Western society, but argues that *all* illness is a form of deviancy, and in this respect mental illness is no different from others. In the course of his discussion Sedgwick raises several important issues, but his analysis is incomplete, so incomplete in fact that it may render some of his conclusions spurious. Nowhere in his deliberation is the difference between *experiencing* a physical and a mental illness examined. It may well be, and most probably is, that the difference between contracting pneumonia, for example, and having a nervous breakdown is such that it calls for widely divergent responses.[6] Still, Sedgwick has a point in bringing to our attention that the distinctions between physical and mental illness which are at the core of Szasz's and Goffman's analyses (but not Laing's and Foucault's) are simplistic. And it is important that he reminds us that it is necessary to examine the wider notion of illness.

In the chapters that follow the chief theoreticians of anti-psychiatry are all in turn castigated for their shortcomings. Goffman is dismissed for his distinction between 'organism' and 'person' following which he separates physical and mental illness. He is also criticized for his notion of a 'total institution' which confuses micro- and macrosocial structures. Thomas Szasz is exposed as a right-wing libertarian, whose contractual psychiatry shows disturbing affinities with the Darwinian sociology of Herbert Spencer and goes hand in hand with the laissez-faire ideology of Ronald Reagan and Margaret Thatcher. Michel Foucault is taken to task for romanticizing his anti-psychiatric vision of a 'dialogue with Unreason' and in the process inaccurately handling historical fact.

The most extensive treatment – two chapters – is reserved for Laing. Laing's post-Ceylon career proved such a disappointment to Sedgwick that he can no longer bear to think anything positive about the earlier phase of Laing's work. Now there are no redeeming features in the Laingian project. The first chapter is a reprint of the 1971 article but with two modifications. First the title changes – now it is called 'The

Radical Trip' – and, second, all the favourable comments that we find in
it are removed (which is different from actually re-evaluating the work).
The second chapter concentrates on Laing's post-Ceylon period. The
picture is very depressing; Laing's downfall was simply too much. We
find there an account of Laing's involvement in Leboyean birth
ideology. We also get the full list of his backtrackings – no, he did not
consider himself an anti-psychiatrist but a psychiatrist; no, he did not
go along with the radical left. Finally, Sedgwick assesses the results of
the Kingsley Hall experience and concludes that the possibility of
emerging from a psychosis in a creative way is doubtful: 'the years of
practice have led not to a cumulation of evidence and theory but to a
growing inconclusiveness' (Sedgwick 1982:119).

And as for the activities of the other communities of The
Philadelphia Association Sedgwick thinks that they do no more than
other similar organizations – they arrange for housing psychiatric
patients rather than healing them.

Sedgwick's denunciation of anti-psychiatry is merciless. He leaves no
stone unturned in seeking out the failings of the movement. Many of his
observations are important, particularly his analysis of the libertarian
free-market psychiatry as envisaged by Szasz; there is always a need to
remind the public that some of the rhetoric of freedom conceals a wish
to return to a Darwinian society. But while almost all criticisms are
pertinent there is also something disquieting about the tone – disdain,
scorn, mockery, curt dismissal. After all, these thinkers have helped
enormously in alerting the public to the issues of psychiatry, even if
ideologically some of them are not acceptable. (Probably all anti-
psychiatrists were aware of Szasz's political views, which did not stop
them from acknowledging their debt to his work, possibly much to
Szasz's annoyance.)

But it is not only an ideological concern that animates Sedgwick's
denunciation. Because of a personal concern, which he openly
mentions in the book (his adoptive mother withered away in an
appalling ward for chronic schizophrenics), he will not accept any
theory or practice which will not address the problem of chronic
schizophrenics. And certainly, from this perspective the ideas of
'contracting a psychiatrist', 'dialogue with Unreason' or a 'psychotic
voyage' are at best irrelevant. Sedgwick is right in pointing out that a
psychiatric practice which does not concern itself with the straightforward question of care for those who are incapable of looking after
themselves is inadequate, whatever its ideological affinity. Sedgwick is

just as right to insist that psychiatry must ultimately be a comprehensive response of the society. But often his arguments reduce the problem to the question of dealing with the mentally disabled, without ever analysing how people get to the stage of chronic disablement. Should Sedgwick attempt such an analysis he would probably be hampered by his opening premise that there is no essential difference between mental and physical illness. Such an analysis would probably also necessitate an acceptance of some of the arguments that came from the 'anti-psychiatric' quarters.

Sedgwick is not only preoccupied with a negative critique, he also presents an alternative to existing psychiatry. However, the choice of model is positively bizarre, at least as far as his account of it goes. Sedgwick opts for the longstanding experiment of the Belgian village of Geel which has its beginnings in medieval times, 1250 to be precise, and which was much admired by Kropotkin. From the beginning Geel functioned as a centre for pilgrimage and settlement for the mentally afflicted. This tradition of admitting the mentally ill into the community has survived to this day. In its modern version it is supervised by medical authorities who screen those who are sent there, excluding violent and difficult cases. Once accepted, such a person will enter a household and most likely will remain there for the rest of his/her life. It sounds really wonderful except that Sedgwick's description contains one or two details that make one doubt that this is really the ideal for community care.

> The remuneration of the host-hostels from public sources of support is of course a *sine qua non* of any family-care boarding system of the disabled. Aside from a certain degree of economic exploitation as cheap farming and domestic labour (extremely difficult to check where members of the family are involved in such a labour as a matter of normal expectation), the patients are received into care at Geel in a spirit which transcends any attribution of either selfishness or of altruism to their hosts.
>
> (Sedgwick 1982:255)

Maybe. But when we learn about some other conditions imposed on those admitted into community care then we really begin to wonder.

> There is a strict prohibition of sexual contact. That, and the rather extensive limiting of unaccompanied excursions into the town itself (affecting some two-thirds of these patients), constitutes the entire

extent of formal bureaucratic regulation of the patients' freedom of movement.

(ibid.:254)

To see prohibition of sexual contact and virtual house arrest, for those already screened by medical authorities as not dangerous or difficult, described as the 'entire' extent of control, without any pause for reflection on what this may really mean, makes one's mind boggle. One can only repeat to Sedgwick words he used at one point in relation to Laing – 'the blindness of these passages is unbelievable' (ibid.:87). Sedgwick refers to himself as a 'revolutionary-socialist writer and teacher, trained in the earliest and the most recent battles of the post-war New Left' (ibid.:243), but it seems that such ideological purity is no guarantee of a sound analysis.

This is stranger still in view of the fact that Sedgwick does not reserve any of the energy he spent in denouncing Goffman, Szasz, Foucault and Laing for an examination of the Italian model, both in its theoretical stance and the actual practice, though it is evident from his book that he knew it well. It is strange because it would seem, at least at first glance, that the Italians would meet many of Sedgwick's requirements – they had a high level of political awareness, they involved the whole community in their work, and there is nothing that would prevent them from setting up a structure of genuine care where it was needed. But then this would mean that Sedgwick would have to accept some of the anti-psychiatric ideology into his reasoning and this, it seems, he simply could not bring himself to do.

IV

Peter Sedgwick was not the only critic who came from the ranks of the left. Another harsh look at Laing's work came from Russell Jacoby, an historian closely linked to Herbert Marcuse and the Frankfurt School. In the book *Social Amnesia. A Critique of Contemporary Psychology from Adler to Laing*, which came out in 1975, Jacoby reviews the psychoanalytically oriented theories – the 'New-Freudians' and the 'Post-Freudians'. Laing is put in the latter category. On one level this is justified. Laing had trained as a psychoanalyst, and in his earlier work, mostly *The Divided Self*, he was much influenced by psychoanalytical thought. On another level it does not make a great deal of sense to put Laing in this lineage as the stakes of his work were altogether different. Laing did come via psychoanalysis but was going somewhere else.

It also puts Laing in the same bracket as some other American psychotherapists and authors such as Abraham Maslow and Carl Rogers for whom he himself had little respect.[7] However, it has to be said that Jacoby is well aware of the differences between the non-political liberal humanists and the more politically minded thinkers like Laing. Another unfortunate feature of this critique is that Laing is discussed together with Cooper as though they were speaking with the same voice. In this instance, this does not lead to any serious misrepresentations, but a commentary at this level should not conflate the work of two independent thinkers, however similar their views may at times be.

A theme which runs throughout the book, and which is applied with rigorous force to Laing, is that the revisions of the new post-Freudian and post-Marxist theoreticians weaken the hard subversive edge which is the strength of the original theories. This weakening happens through the 'humanizing' tendencies of these new developments. In the case of the re-workings of Freud, particularly in the American versions, this happens through the insertion of the interpersonal dimension into the theory, which renders the theory perhaps more 'common sense' but less radical. In the particular case of Laing, his attachment to Feuerbach's I–You philosophy is the case in point. Marx criticized Feuerbach because his social reality was reduced to a timeless human encounter and Jacoby contends that this critique is just as relevant to Laing.

> The confusion between the surface and the essence leads Laing and Cooper to make the elementary bourgeois error: they mistake the phenomenon specific to one historical era as universal and invariant. In brief, they take the human relations that prevail in the late bourgeois society as human relations as such . . . When Laing says that 'human beings are constantly thinking about others and about what others are thinking about them, and what others think they are thinking about the others, and so on,' he neglects to add the crucial qualification: not all human beings, but human beings who have been mesmerized and mutilated. 'Human beings' seek double and triple confirmation when the first fails; and the first fails when the ego that advances it fails. The ego, frightened over its own fragility, seeks endless confirmations it can never give nor receive. The logic of human relations approaches the logic of paranoia: in every nook and cranny lurks danger.
>
> (Jacoby 1975:144)

Jacoby further argues that Laing's interpersonal theory of identity is a theory of an impotent identity.

What is lacking in Feuerbach is what is lacking in Laing and Cooper
. . . Because objectification or praxis is lacking in Feuerbach, his
theory, for all its humanism, its I/Thou, is a passive one. It does not
comprehend the world as a social environment, the congealed
product of human praxis. This failure Laing and Cooper share with
Feuerbach; they succumb to the spectacle: the nonactivity of
watching and viewing and being watched.

(ibid.:147)

Another point that Jacoby raises, and which stems from his reading
of Freud, is the relation between theory and therapy. Jacoby admires
Freud for keeping a clear distinction between these two and for
remaining consistent in this. Jacoby thinks this is important and asserts,
in the same vein, that 'there is no such activity as radical therapy – there
is only therapy and radical politics' (ibid.:139). Jacoby does not
demonstrate how this confusion manifests itself in Laing's thought, but
presumably he means the activities of Kingsley Hall. This separation
between therapy and politics is an arresting thought, something worth
bearing in mind, although it is perhaps a bit too neat and it invites the
idea of therapy addressing some pure objective entity which can be
separated from the wider context in which it appears.

Jacoby's commentary is short but useful. The most valuable is his
demonstration of the limitations in Laing's understanding of the social
praxis.

V

As we can see, Laing came in for heavy criticism both from the right
and from the left. Another attack came from the feminists. A little
surprising, perhaps, because one would have thought that although
Laing did not write anything specifically to help the women's cause, he
did not write anything to offend women, either. Not so, according to
Elaine Showalter, a specialist on literature and women's studies, who
ventured into the realm of psychiatry with her book *The Female
Malady. Women, Madness and English Culture, 1830–1980*. The work
is intended as a 'feminist history of psychiatry and a cultural history of
madness as a female malady' (Showalter 1987:5) and it concentrates, as
the sub-title indicates, on developments that took place in England. The
main thesis of the book is that 'madness' and 'femininity' have been
throughout defined in terms of a male norm, through a male-dominated
profession. Showalter remarks, with justification, that the radical

historians of madness, beginning with Foucault, have neglected this dimension in their analyses. One could add to her argument that in the accounts of psychiatric abuse, those singled out as being suppressed geniuses are invariably men (Van Gogh, Hölderlin, Nietzsche, Artaud, etc.) but never women. Showalter intends to redress the balance.

The careers of four key figures of English psychiatry are scrutinized – the Victorian John Conolly, who was famed for his non-restraint work in Hanwell Asylum; Henry Maudsley, founder of the Maudsley Hospital, a representative of Darwinian psychiatry (a term Showalter borrows from Vieda Skultans (Skultans 1975)); W.H.R. Rivers, active during World War I, one of the first importers of Freud's theories to England and probably best known for his therapeutic work with Siegfried Sassoon; and R.D. Laing. Towards the end of the chapter about Laing – the last in the book – Showalter states that it is impossible to write about Laing's work 'without acknowledging the importance of his analysis of madness as a female strategy within the family. For a whole generation of women, Laing's work was a significant validation of perceptions that found little social support elsewhere' (ibid.:246). However, nothing in Showalter's presentation bears any of this acknowledgement. In fact, she goes on to say that the 'movement' came perilously close to exploiting its women patients. To this effect she quotes David Cooper whom she describes as 'the most politically radical of the Kingsley Hall group' (ibid.:247) (Cooper was not involved in Kingsley Hall; he was at the time running the Villa 21 project). The quote comes from his *The Grammar of Living*, a book he wrote when he was in the grip of a Reichian belief in the healing properties of the orgasm. In it he speaks of the value of 'bed therapy' with his patients and claimed that he could detect a 'non-orgasmic personality' by 'minute ocular deflections and by sentences spoken to one that fail to connect because they are never properly ended' (ibid.:247). Such views are sexist and extremely offensive but they are not Laing's, and he cannot be held responsible for them. Nevertheless, this quote and a further few remarks on Cooper's views come immediately after the few words of praise, cited above, and they round off the chapter dealing with Laing's work.

But this is not the worst of it. Showalter constructs her major argument around a serious misrepresentation. Because of her commitment to the idea that the male psychiatrist bases his power on a female patient, Showalter presents Mary Barnes as 'Laing's only complete case study' (ibid.:232), an assertion that only a cursory glance at Laing's writings and Mary Barnes's book shows to be false. Laing did live for a year in the same community as Mary Barnes and his influence was enormous, but at least four other therapists had more to do with her than Laing himself – Joseph Berke, her principal therapist; Aaron Esterson, who was for a year her therapist while she was waiting for Kingsley Hall to open; Noel Cobb and Paul Zeal, who joined the community later and worked a great deal with her. No extra research, or inside knowledge, is needed for this information; it is all in Mary Barnes's book. It does not matter. Showalter sticks to her thesis and refers to Laing's 'many discussions of Mary Barnes' (ibid.:235), without giving any references, or says that he 'made most of Mary Barnes's "recovery"' (ibid.:235) without explaining how. And the references are missing because she would not find any. The only time Laing mentions Mary Barnes is in the little-known paper, 'Metanoia: Some Experiences at Kingsley Hall' (Laing 1968) written well before she was a celebrity. Showalter neither refers to it nor mentions it in the bibliography (though one has to assume that she has read it as the book in which the paper later appeared (Ruitenbeek 1972) does appear in the bibliography). But Showalter does not need references. She ploughs on regardless with the kind of certainty which comes from knowing in advance.

> I suspect that her [Mary Barnes's] voyage was unlike his expecta-
> tions. It was one thing to relive the dangerous exhilaration of his
> mountain-climbing experiences in Scotland, and to be the manly
> physician priest leading another explorer to the heart of darkness, or
> the top of Everest, five days in, five days out. It was quite another to
> spend three years changing diapers, giving bottles, and generally
> wiping up after a noisy, jealous, smelly, middle-aged woman. The
> image of the schizophrenic voyage that Laing had created drew upon
> his own heroic fantasies; it was a male adventure of exploration and
> conquest – scarcely the reality of Mary Barnes's experience. Faced
> with the obligation to play mother on the psychic journey, Laing
> seems to have lost enthusiasm for it.
>
> (ibid.:235–236)

This portrayal of Laing is a concoction of insinuation, rampant prejudice and distortion of fact. It is significant that in putting together the picture of Laing Showalter draws heavily on fictionalized accounts such as Erica Jong's *Fear of Flying* and Clancy Sigal's *Zone of the Interior*. Passages like the one just cited, and one could quote more, make one wonder if it is possible to take seriously the claim that the book is a 'feminist history of psychiatry' because if the remainder of the book is of the same quality as the chapter dealing with Laing (and this is not the place to undertake a detailed analysis of the entire book) then the prospects are not very encouraging. On the other hand it has to be said that the book contains plenty of interesting primary source material and is in many respects useful.

Strangest of all, considering that Showalter's work purports to speak for women, is her treatment of Mary Barnes, as rarely has she been portrayed with less sympathy and respect. This particularly applies to the description of Mary Barnes's life after her stay at Kingsley Hall. We are told that some years later, on the occasion of the London première of the play *Mary Barnes* by David Edgar, she appeared a 'lisping, bouncing, and giggling fifty-five-year-old woman, who acted in a beguiling child-like way' (ibid.:236). We also learn that she admitted to a reporter from the *Guardian* that she was still wrestling with acute attacks of depression and withdrawal. This is all we get about the post-Kingsley Hall Mary Barnes. Of course, it is necessary for Showalter's thesis that she was a victim. She is described as 'Laing's only complete case, his Augustine, his Dora, his Anna O' (ibid.:232) (Augustine, Dora and Anna O. were the famous cases of Charcot, Freud and Breuer, respectively). And so, while all the male psychiatrists are representatives of the same repressive order, so are all their women patients the same – victims.[8] But Mary Barnes was no victim. She had her 'voyage' well worked out in her head long before she met Laing. Of course, one can view her 'recovery' whichever way one chooses and, as with any treatment, one is entitled to question whether she would have not got better without the benefits of the stay at Kingsley Hall. But in a way recover she did. After the community she never took any psychotropic drugs again, she fervently believed that she could be of help to others, she was always willing to give this help, she was well liked, and yes, she did from time to time go through 'downs'. But when we compare the medicated, battered by electroshock treatment woman with the essentially happy, if quite eccentric, Mary Barnes after Kingsley Hall, then we should certainly take note. Strange that Showalter, who judging from the acknowledgments to her book interviewed quite a number of people, never took the trouble to actually interview Mary Barnes who was easy to get hold of and usually quite willing to speak about her experiences.

There is obviously every good reason for subjecting Laing's views to an analysis from a feminist point of view, but any such undertaking has to follow a basic sense of fairness, some rudimentary appreciation of the theoretical position, and respect for the facts. This is not the case in this instance. Intriguingly a few of the features of Showalter's exposé remind one of Thomas Szasz's. Szasz referred to Mary Barnes as Laing's Wolf-woman and he put her into a lineage of 'famous cases'; he also quotes Cooper in his case against Laing; there is even the same image of a Laingian psychotic voyage as an Alpinistic trip, and last but not least, they are both basically character assassinations. Showalter does not mention Szasz's paper so no doubt these similarities are a coincidence. Ordinarily, one would not devote so much time to this kind of presentation, but because of the growing importance of feminist thinking, because of Elaine Showalter's considerable reputation, and because her book went into two reprints, one fears that this account may be taken by many women as authoritative. This would be a shame.

VI

Elaine Showalter was not the first feminist to respond to Laing. In 1974, Juliet Mitchell published *Psychoanalysis and Feminism* in which a few chapters deal with Laing's ideas. Mitchell's commentary deals exclusively with Laing's theoretical position and sticks closely to the text; it is also quite dense and therefore difficult to summarize.

To begin with, Mitchell concentrates on Laing's ever-pervading notion of 'experience'. She notes that the meaning of the term changes and she identifies three ways in which it appears: there is a *science* of experience, a *politics* of experience, and a *mystico-religious* pursuit of transcendental experience. She also draws attention to two other ways in which Laing uses the term 'experience', which are often contradictory and mutually exclusive.

> 'Experience' as a noun is thus Laing's existential, essentialist 'existence' – always 'true' – and 'experience' as a verb is to perceive or conceive of something and these conceptions can play us true or false.
>
> What we have then is a background of 'experience' (noun) as 'true experience' (easily merging into 'transcendental experience') and a foreground of 'experience' (verb) of how one perceives (conceives one's own and the other's behaviour).
>
> (Mitchell 1974:243)

Mitchell shows that, for all his opposition to the psychoanalytical notion of a separate person, Laing remains just as entrenched in this position as he keeps the locus of 'true' experience within the person. But although for Laing the notion of a 'true' experience is important, in reality, Mitchell argues, he cannot demonstrate it. What he can demonstrate, and does, is the difference between behaviour and perception of behaviour and document how it degenerates into the infinity of a dyadic spiral as he did in *Knots*.

Another issue that draws Mitchell's attention is Laing's rejection of the 'unconscious' for the notion of visibility and intelligibility, and for his claim that the 'unconscious' is what we do not communicate, to ourselves, or to one another. Mitchell comments: 'to Laing it [the unconscious] can be understood (rendered intelligible) in *exactly* the same way as consciousness. It has no different laws – it is quite straightforward, if only we will look at it' (ibid.:255). Mitchell argues that Laing's position leads to unwelcome consequences because if the unconscious is essentially the same as the conscious then there is no clear way of explaining the formation of a neurotic or a psychotic symptom, and so no distinction between 'normal', neurotic and psychotic behaviour is possible. This, in a sense, is indeed the position Laing arrived at. The difference between the neurotic and psychotic, to limit the discussion to the realm of the pathological, lies, Mitchell contends, precisely in processes which are unconscious. Mitchell's position is close to the psychoanalytical orthodoxy in that she views psychosis as having its origins in the narcissistic pre-Oedipal stage, which is also a pre-verbal stage, hence the frequent broken language of a psychotic. Neurosis, on the other hand, has its nucleus in the Oedipus Complex, when the sexed entry of the child into his or her world takes place. Mitchell remarks that Laing obviously does not have to follow the Freudian theory, but the way in which he dissolves all differences she does not find helpful. (She also reminds us, importantly, that Freud was the first to see a continuity between the normal and the pathological but it did not lead him to abolish the difference.)

Yet despite these criticisms, Mitchell is not in a hurry to dismiss Laing.

> Laing's work has the merit of lucidly giving us new (and forgotten old) aspects of the phenomenological terrain for future analysis. Laing places our assumed ideology before our eyes. As the field he is working in directed him consciously to the family and unintentionally to women he gives us some very useful food for thought.
>
> (ibid.:273)

And later on:

after reading Laing's studies we understand much better the internal characteristics of the nuclear family.

(ibid.:285)

The studies that Mitchell has in mind are the family cases in *Sanity, Madness and the Family*, and she finds that a great deal can be learnt from them. These studies are of interest to women because all the accounts, 'by chance', as Mitchell puts it, are of schizophrenic women, and because they centre around the mother–daughter relationship. The stories reveal the particular difficulties that women have in sexual emancipation. Mitchell quotes from Laing and Esterson a typical example:

Spontaneity, especially sexual spontaneity, is the very heart of subversion to institutional mores, to pre-set role taking and assigning. Spontaneous affection, sexuality, anger, would have shattered Mr. and Mrs. Church's [the parents] shells to bits.

(SMF:99)

If Laing's (and in this instance Esterson's) work is of help to women it is also largely accidental and he does not follow up some important clues that are present in the material. The one issue that stands out is the role of the father. He is absent from these case-studies. In some respects this is quite typical of the pre-Oedipal organization which is characterized by the absence of the Oedipal father. But Mitchell goes on to observe that Laing and Esterson did not deliberately set out to demonstrate this, but if anything, they colluded with it. This is evidenced from the number of interviews conducted with the mother (up to twenty-nine) and with the father (in almost all cases only two).

Of all the commentaries, Juliet Mitchell's is the most thorough, the least emotionally charged, and the least ideologically determined. The way she assesses Laing's work is that his strength was to present a number of problems which had not been clearly articulated before; the weakness was that he did not analyse them adequately. Her critique is more Freudian than feminist, or to put it more precisely, she articulates her disagreements with Laing primarily from the conceptual apparatus of psychoanalysis. It also makes clear why psychoanalysts do not read Laing. However, one does not have to be an adherent of this school of thinking to appreciate the pertinence of Mitchell's reading.

VII

Considering how famous Kingsley Hall was at the time of its existence there are very few extended commentaries on the project. Some of the reactions were somewhat exaggerated. Szasz, on account of many of the community members' left-wing leanings, saw them all as a bunch of communards; Showalter, on account of Kingsley Hall's reputation of being connected with the London counter-culture, presented it as one of those wild partying scenes. Many psychiatrists and psychotherapists were taking a keen interest in Kingsley Hall's activities but no extended appreciations followed, mostly because it was a short-lived experiment and for lack of any material (theoretical writings, statistics, etc.) to chew on. Those who did comment almost invariably, and understandably, focused on Mary Barnes; her book was after all the major source on the community's activities. The dismissals (as opposed to critiques) of the 'case of Mary Barnes' proceeded along two different routes. The first was simply to rubbish the story by focusing on its sensationalism and Laing's supposed exploitation of it. The second was to question the case's clinical worth on the grounds that it was misdiagnosed, i.e., she was not really schizophrenic (usually opting for a diagnosis of hysteria).[9] The origins of this lie in the old view that schizophrenia is incurable, which means that if a 'cure' takes place then it could not have been schizophrenia to begin with. This argument is no longer repeated in such a blunt form, but the fact that the value of a case can be diminished by simply challenging the diagnosis points to it.

There have been a few, though not many, more considered comments about Kingsley Hall. The most interesting came from the Continental anti-psychiatrists. Félix Guattari, the French psychoanalyst (or perhaps lapsed psychoanalyst as he developed a fiercely anti-Freudian rhetoric) and philosopher, very active at La Borde clinic,[10] criticized the case of Mary Barnes for its slavish repetition of psychoanalytical structures, which in turn reinforced the parental order of the community (Guattari 1984). The other comments came as early as 1967 during the proceedings of the Conference for the Dialectics of Liberation where Giovanni Jervis, of the Italian *Psichiatria Democratica*, expressed his reservations about Kingsley Hall's political position. He argued that by setting up a community within the private independent mode, the community's impact on the wider problem, society's use of psychiatric intervention as a repressive force, would be very limited if at all effective. He predicted that by eschewing a more direct political stance

Kingsley Hall would become marginalized (Jervis 1967). Time has shown that his prediction was correct.

Another book which had considerable impact was an account of a woman's psychosis which had gone horribly wrong. *Anna* (Reed 1979), written by the husband of the woman in question, tells a painful story of how after several attempts at overcoming her psychosis by living through it, she ended in burning herself to death. Laing himself was not much involved, but he makes two fleeting appearances in the book. On one occasion, 'Anna's' husband meets him on the street; he seeks some explanation about his wife's predicament but all that Laing can say is that twenty years earlier he knew better how people came back from a psychosis than he does now (Reed 1979:69). Interestingly, Mary Barnes also comes onto the scene, and at a very crucial moment. At one point, rather suddenly, 'Anna' becomes lucid; from one moment to the next all the signs of psychosis disappear. Mary Barnes is worried by the suddenness of the 'recovery'. And she is right. The next day 'Anna' turns herself into a human torch.[11]

Laing had less to do with 'Anna' than with Mary Barnes (with the latter he at least lived in the same house for a year) but the book was an account of what some referred to as 'Laingian therapy' and was seen to demonstrate what can happen in the reckless world of 'psychotic voyages'. One commentator, reviewing the history of anti-psychiatry, put it succinctly:

> It is not – for all its insights and intellectual brilliance – Laing's *The Divided Self* that makes the greater impact; rather it is David Reed's *Anna*, the tragic story of an individual schizophrenic who was persuaded by a Laingian doctor to face up to her madness without drugs, and whose slow, painful death from self-inflicted burns symbolizes in the most awful way the end of an era in psychiatry.
>
> (Claridge 1990:157)

VIII

After going through all the commentaries on Laing there does not seem to be anything left. Every aspect of his project has come in for severe criticism. His theoretical thinking is full of inconsistencies; his ideological position (however widely conceived) was too fickle; the practical, i.e. the clinical or therapeutic, value of his work is uncertain, to say the least. The only work that escaped criticism is *The Divided*

Self. By common agreement this is Laing's finest achievement; nothing that followed had quite the same quality. One may agree with this view or not, but it is easy to see where it comes from. *The Divided Self* is to this day the finest existential analysis, at least in English, of what it means to go mad. Two other works also deserve to remain on most reading lists. The first is *Sanity, Madness and the Family*. The criticisms levelled against it have made us aware of some of the limitations of the book but these have not diminished its value, they have simply tightened the book's boundaries. Otherwise the work still remains one of the best presentations of what happens in families. The other book is *The Politics of Experience*, because, if nothing else, it is an important document of the era.

But Laing has not influenced in any appreciable way either psychiatrists, or psychoanalysts, or the wider net of theoreticians. And yet, and yet. The phenomenon of Laing did leave something behind. Some of it is quite tangible, some less so.

The divergence of the critique of Laing also attests to the breadth of his appeal. Many who were attracted to him were so disappointed, to the point of feeling betrayed, by his post-Kingsley Hall career that they stopped considering Laing at all seriously. Others did not take much note (or did not know much) of the later career of Laing, and to them it was rather that he slowly disappeared from the scene. So some changed their minds about Laing, some simply have forgotten him. The odd references that still occasionally appear are usually of an historic nature, that is, he is mentioned as a founder of a short-lived movement that has petered away. Sometimes, however, he is given unusually strong credit in quite unexpected places. A psychoanalyst, Nina Coltart, who had been closely involved with The Arbours Association (an off-shoot of The Philadelphia Association) summed up Laing's influence in the following way:

> What was revolutionary about the early work of R.D. Laing, and people like our Joe Berke and Morty Schatzman, was that prolonged, careful and human attention was payed to trying to make sense, in context, of what was happening to a mad patient. I am not implying that psychoanalysis did not do this. It was Freud's great contribution to the twentieth century that in 1895 he started doing just that; but, with very rare exceptions, psychoanalysts have worked with neurotic patients. Psychotic disturbance has usually been considered beyond its scope. The distinctive innovation which Laing, himself a psychoanalyst, brought to analytical therapy was to

direct the attention of the technique of psychoanalysis to
psychotically disordered people, on a holistic basis.

(Coltart 1995:159–160)

Coming from a psychoanalyst this may seem a somewhat curious
statement. It is true that psychoanalysis began as a therapeutic method
for neurosis, and it is just as true that Freud himself did not see much
promise in its application to psychosis. But within the ranks of
psychoanalysis, both close to Freud and in America, inroads into the
world of the psychotic were being made long before Laing came onto
the scene. Harry Stack Sullivan, Frieda Fromm-Reichmann, John
Rosen, Paul Federn, Harold Searles are the few names that come to
mind. What is in a way even more curious is that Laing would probably
not recognize himself in this praise – he did not see himself as someone
contributing to the psychoanalytical body of knowledge. But although
curious these comments do make sense because, while indeed there
were others before Laing, he put across the message that psychotics can
be helped with an unprecedented force. Furthermore, he did not claim,
as psychoanalysts usually did, and sometimes still do, that this work has
to be done with a medical back-up. This back-up would operate as a
kind of safety net for the analyst, giving him the option of advising/
requesting hospitalization of a patient. In a set-up like this the analyst is
still effectively the agent of the hospital (this is more common in the US
where psychoanalysts are often also practising psychiatrists). Finally,
Coltart also adds the important rider – this new approach that came with
Laing is characterized by a 'holistic basis'. This is a reference to the
work of various therapeutic communities that followed after Kingsley
Hall. Coltart had been involved with The Arbours Association for
several years and these remarks about Laing appear in a publication
presenting the work of the organization (hence 'our' Joe Berke and
Morty Schatzman in the quote above). Coming in this context what
Coltart has to say about Laing is not at all curious.

The therapeutic communities are the most tangible legacy of
Laing's work. After Kingsley Hall ended, The Philadelphia Association and The Arbours Association made the running of these
communities an integral part of their activities. The communities of
today are very different from Kingsley Hall. Probably the best way of
describing the changes would be to point out the increased importance
of the psychoanalytical ethos of the communities. This is understandable as both The Philadelphia Association and The Arbours
Association have become part of the psychoanalytically oriented

psychotherapy mainstream. This is reflected in the way the community therapists engage – they tend to work to strictly arranged and strictly timed meetings. In some houses of The Philadelphia Association these meetings are, with the exception of some serious crises, the sole therapeutic involvement. In such cases one could perhaps speak of community-analysis, a modified form of group-analysis. The Arbours, unlike The Philadelphia Association, still emphasise the role of the therapist as a full living-in member of the community – their psychotherapy training programme requires all trainees to live for six months in a community. In comparison with Kingsley Hall roles are probably far clearer, but the basic principle that the community itself makes the crucial decision on who is in and who is out remains. For a more serious evaluation one would need more reports from those who work in these households.[12]

Apart from these communities virtually nothing of Laing's ideas filtered into the 'official' thinking of social work, psychoanalysis or psychiatry. There has been, however, some 'unofficial' residue. Anthony Clare, the doyen of psychiatry's establishment, interviewed Laing on the radio programme *In the Psychiatrist's Chair*. He preceded the published version of the interview with a very warm and sympathetic introduction. After a three-page fair scan of Laing's career he concluded with the following:

> His was a powerful voice in the movement to demystify mental illness and he undoubtedly contributed to the process whereby psychiatry moved out of the large, isolated, grim mental hospitals into acute units attached to general hospitals and into the community. His own therapeutic community at Kingsley Hall served as a prototype for many similar non-hospital settings for people in psychological crises. He challenged the crude reductionism in psychiatry which had followed the enthusiastic introduction of the powerful antidepressant and antipsychotic drugs. He influenced a whole generation of young men and women in their choice of psychiatry as a career.
>
> Of course his extraordinarily powerful Glaswegian rhetoric led to overkill and many relatives struggling to cope with seriously mentally ill patients still find it hard to forgive him for seeming to suggest that they were responsible for the very condition they attempted to manage . . . [But] in a particular sense, everyone in contemporary psychiatry owes something to R.D. Laing and,

whatever the profound shortcomings in his life-long argument about the nature of mental illness, he at all times demanded that the plight of the mentally ill be taken absolutely seriously.

(Clare 1992:204–205)

Whether many other psychiatrists feel similarly about Laing is hard to tell.

IX

The response to Laing amounts to a mixture of outright rejection, considered criticism and occasional warm praise. But the questions raised by Laing and the other anti-psychiatrists still remain. They put on the map the issue of the relation between madness and power. And although today this debate may not be very prominent, the problem has not gone away.

All anti-psychiatrists agreed that the power of the traditional hospital was repressive, although opinion varied on how to respond to it. The tactics ranged from experimental wards within the confines of a large hospital (Villa 21), to independent communities (Kingsley Hall), to guerilla tactics (SPK), to reform of the entire system (*Psichiatria Democratica*). But another more complex argument went on. It concerned the nature of madness. All agreed that classical psychiatric understanding of madness only perpetuates the madperson's alienation. All (with the exception of some of the French anti-psychiatrists) rejected psychoanalysis. Two different solutions dominated the debate: first, madness was viewed as a reflection of our system – the family, the psychiatric institution, the society on the whole (SPK, the Italians, Laing); second, madness was conceived as a primary force, where some ancient truths can be found, and this madness points to a reality radically different from our grey normality (Cooper, Foucault, sometimes Laing). Out of these positions several ways of rendering the relation between power and madness emerged. SPK and the Italians sought to transform the oppressed class (the patients) into a force of change. In Germany it took a more extreme form; the principal publication of SPK was significantly entitled *To Turn Illness into a Weapon (Aus der Krankheit eine Waffe Machen)*. Another route was proposed by David Cooper – he elevated madness to the status of a liberatory force. It is useful to clarify somewhat Cooper's position, not only because many of these views were attributed to Laing, but also because in drawing the differences between Laing and Cooper some further issues can be clarified. Here are a few typical utterances from *The Language of Madness* (Cooper 1980):

> Madness is permanent revolution in the life of a person. Sometimes this revolutionary process becomes evident as a major change in the way that we live, a change in the direction of greater autonomy that may be accomplished without the intervention of other people, but sometimes it becomes socially visible as a crisis in which other people intervene.
>
> (Cooper 1980:37)

> Madness is another [need to cancel out all the alienated forms of existence], but madness not as some sort of tragic personal crisis but as renewal of oneself in a way that breaks all obsessional rules of what we have to be but at the same time hurts no one; madness as a deconstitution of oneself with the implicit promise of return to a more fully realized world.
>
> (ibid.:51)

> Madness, presently, is universal subversion desperately chased by extending systems of control and surveillance. It will find its issue with the victory of all forms of subversive struggle against capitalism, fascism and imperialism and against the massive, undigested lumps of repression that exist in bureaucratic socialism, awaiting the social revolution that got left behind in the urgency of political revolution, understandably perhaps, but never excusably.
>
> (ibid.:149)

Cooper distinguishes between 'schizophrenia' and madness. The former is a construct of the bourgeois psychiatry, the latter is an inherent revolutionary force. Once genuine madness asserts itself schizophrenia will cease to exist. So what is this madness? It seems it can be any form of dissent that breaks down the existing bourgeois structures. For example, orgasm is also madness ('Orgasm is a contagious, good madness' (ibid.:74)) because it contradicts the bourgeois procreative sexuality. But why call all these acts of dissent madness? Presumably because they are meant to act on one's consciousness, pushing it to a realm which transcends normality. Madness is universal force.[13]

The idea that in some individuals a creative force manifests itself in a form which seems like madness goes back to the ancient Greeks, but Cooper elevates this force to the universal dimension which bears all the hallmarks of the Hegelian Spirit: 'The future of madness is its end, its transformation into universal creativity which is the lost place where it came from in the first place' (ibid.:149).

The attribution of Cooper's views to Laing led to accusations that he romanticized madness, that he held the mad to be bearers of a new light, and that he even encouraged people to have psychotic experiences. Laing did not hold these views. He only went so far as to say that some people get through a psychotic breakdown without a psychiatric intervention; he thought that this intervention can be detrimental, hence the project of Kingsley Hall; he also said that sometimes in some psychotic breakdowns there may be a sign of a mystical experience, and this is definitely fair enough, especially if we remember that some psychiatrists would be liable to consider mystical experiences as the same as psychotic experiences. However, it is one thing to accept that some people have mystical experiences, but it is another to argue that mysticism can be a force of social liberation, a view which Laing never held either. (One can, of course, doubt whether such a thing as a 'mystical experience' exists, but this would fly in the face of too many testimonies.)

Laing did, however, set out to re-evaluate our notion of what is considered a mental illness. This was already present, although only tacitly, in *The Divided Self*. Later it developed into a comprehensive line of reasoning. He was pitching his arguments against psychiatry's prevailing view that between insanity and normality there is an unbridgeable gap.

> Psychiatrists never tire of telling us that there is an unbridgeable gulf between some people and the rest of us. Karl Jaspers called it an abyss of difference. No human bond can span it. Some people are 'strange, puzzling, inconceivable, uncanny, incapable of empathy, sinister, frightening; it is impossible to approach them as equals', in Manfred Bleuler's words. Both he and Jaspers are talking about schizophrenia – over one in ten of us according to orthodox psychiatry.
>
> (WMF:6)

From this point of view Juliet Mitchell's reproach to Laing that he collapses the difference between schizophrenia and normality is less important (though it remains valid within her, that is psychoanalytical, system of reference) as Laing not so much collapses the difference but opens a different perspective. It is in this context that we should read what he wrote in the Preface to the Pelican edition of *The Divided Self*: 'I am still writing in this book too much about Them, and too little about Us' (DS:11).

While re-evaluating our understanding of madness Laing came to conclude that 'normality' is a sham. Having thus stated this problem, Laing runs into a difficulty. He rejects our notion of normality, but he cannot elevate madness to a liberatory force the way Cooper did. There seem to be two reasons for this. First, during his years working in hospitals, Laing had seen enough of the destruction caused by schizophrenia to make it impossible to seriously consider such a line (hence, so often, he spoke of the wretchedness of psychosis, or of a death-in-life existence). Second, it is clear from Laing's analyses that schizophrenia is a product, so to speak, of the bourgeois reality, not a voice of an independent force through which one can find liberation.

However, in stating his distaste for the prevalent notion of normality and showing at the same time a definite empathy with those who are described as psychotic, Laing invited the conclusion that Cooper made, but he himself did not make it. The question remains. How to escape the unpalatable choice, between the grey and numbing normality and the wretchedness of madness?

This question was addressed very interestingly by Giovanni Jervis. He rejects the idea of madness as a liberatory force as he is of the view that those that psychiatrists face are first and foremost people who have been mutilated by our bourgeois normality, not prophets of new sanity. Jervis thinks that a breakdown may well be an attempt to break out of an unlivable situation but that it usually ends in a bad 're-fall' into normality. He agrees that there may be illuminating experiences in psychosis but he does not think that it is a state to be sought. In this respect his position is quite close to Laing's. He also points out that those who have succeeded in negotiating a breakdown creatively *never* want to repeat the experience. (One is reminded that even Jesse Watkins, whose story Laing told in *The Politics of Experience*, did not want to repeat his relatively mild 'ten day voyage': 'I'd be afraid of entering it again' (PE:132).) Jervis further argues that the slogans of this supposedly liberatory madness – 'authenticity of being', 'total freedom of the subject' – have their provenance in the bourgeois ideology. And so in place of the 'false consciousness' of the bourgeoisie we get the 'false freedom' of madness. Finally, Jervis accepts that madness has to be in a sense re-admitted into normality, but he also points to another overlooked direction: should we not conceive of an alternative normality? In the ideology of anti-psychiatry the word 'normality' is so laden with negative connotations that such an idea may sound almost perverse. But the point of it is that it puts the problem into a collective frame (rather than some post-madness sanity which is always an individual act), although perhaps the term 'health' would be better, as it does not evoke the idea of a 'norm'. Jervis does not suggest that anyone knows, right now, what this alternative, sane normality could be like. Addressing the question of normality must be just as complex as the question of madness but Jervis has no doubt that it is principally a political question.[14]

For Laing, who found himself torn between the unacceptable normality and the madness which this normality breeds, re-thinking our notions of 'normality' or 'health' should seem a natural choice. But his own theoretical position makes it very difficult. Some critics (particularly Jacoby) pointed out that Laing viewed interpersonal violence as a fixed, almost eternal, feature of human relations. This is a consequence of the duality that lies behind virtually all of Laing's writings. On the one hand, we find the authentic, the true, the genuine; on the other hand, we find the false, the normal, the ordinary. The first is internal (and only rarely shows itself); the second is external (softened with an imaginary You, which never emerges). Within this scheme re-thinking normality cannot be undertaken. Yet for an anti-psychiatrist this should be an issue just as urgent as re-thinking madness. In this sense, Laing's project only went half-way.

X

Since Laing's days many things have changed. Britain has seen a massive move to the right. The change in the political climate contributed as much to the disappearance of Laing's ideas as his own withdrawal. Suddenly, under the barrage of the new ideology, the left wing and all other alternative groups were in retreat. The reversal of values has been so wide that one cannot even begin to describe it. This has affected the work with the mentally ill which has to conform with the gathering pace of the government's 'Community Care' programme. Patients are leaving 'large, isolated, grim mental hospitals' and going 'into acute units attached to general hospitals and into the community. His [Laing's] own therapeutic community at Kingsley Hall served as a prototype for many similar non-hospital settings for people in psychological crises' (Clare 1992:204).

This is how Anthony Clare describes the current situation. He warmly praises Laing, but his picture of the new community care system sounds far too optimistic. At any rate, in a society which is governed by a slogan, 'There is no such thing as society, there are only individuals', the term 'community care' makes no sense. It is enough to see how social workers were treated to make this plain. It is a revealing example because one would think that social workers should play a crucial role in any 'community care' programme. They were not well prepared. They were poorly trained, they worked to impossible briefs, some of which they set themselves, and they made blunders. All this goes without saying. But what made matters worse (from the point of view of the new ideologues) was that social work drew many with left-wing leanings. So rather than seeing some efforts towards improving their services the social workers were ridiculed, abused, denigrated. Now they are reduced to managers who 'purchase' services, as the current parlance would have it. Those at the receiving end (the mentally ill, the mentally handicapped, the physically handicapped, the elderly, etc.) are referred to as 'consumers' or 'customers'. Inmates in the new private prisons will no doubt be called 'customers', too. The once quite independent organizations which used to run therapeutic communities as they saw fit are more and more affected by this new climate. They now all belong in one pool (market) of services which can be 'purchased' in endless deals that are being struck between various organizations. This is not a time favourable for independent activity.

However, one phenomenon, relatively new, bears the direct imprint of the work of Laing and other anti-psychiatrists – it is the emergence of self-help groups. These bring together the patients, or sufferers, into organized forms of fighting for decent treatment, for respect and for the civil and legal rights of the patients. The first such organization was the Mental Patients' Union (MPU) which was set up in 1973. Currently the strongest organization seems to be Survivors Speak Out. There are many others, some staying for longer periods, some short-lived. For over ten years now the magazine *Asylum* has been a regular forum for these groups.[15] The emergence of these initiatives is not just due to the activities of the anti-psychiatrists; others, such as MIND, have been crucial on organizational and legal terms. And it is important that the patients organize. However well a psychiatric system is worked out there will always be a possible conflict of interest between the professionals and the patients, in a sense not dissimilar to the perpetual tension between the employer and the employed. And just as psychiatrists, nurses, etc., are organized, so should be the patients. Not everyone likes this idea.

Laing was one of those who gave the mentally ill, the patients, the 'psychiatrized', a voice. The force and imagination of his plea helped the sufferers speak out. Perhaps this is Laing's most tangible legacy. In a way it would be quite fitting – he always cared more for the patients than for his fellow professionals. Laing opened up, even if only for a short spell, a horizon which was not there before. There is nothing mysterious about this horizon; it is not about Laing's attempts to convey his glimpses into a transcendental reality. It came from his ability to speak across the barrier, from the professional to the sufferer. In this sense his writings were really a bridge between the 'normal' and the 'mad'. For a variety of reasons the bridge is not there any more but the fact that it once was may perhaps again set aspirations. Of course, one can just reject all this as humbug. It is all about the choices we make. As one commentator on Laing put it, it is either 'a matter of signs and portents [or] a sinister and growing reality' (Britton 1974:30).

NOTES

1 One interview with Laing which appeared at the height of his fame had the following title: 'After Freud and Jung, Now Comes R.D. Laing Pop-Shrink Rebel, Yogi, Philosopher King, Latest Reincarnation of Aesculapius, Maybe' (Mezan 1972).

2 These were mostly money-spinning tours that Laing apparently hated (Mullan 1995:349).

3 Amongst other works Szasz's collection of accounts of psychiatric abuse (real as well as from literature), *The Age of Madness* (Szasz 1974), is particularly helpful.

4 Szasz founded the American Association for the Abolition of Involuntary Mental Hospitalizations.

5 In Italy the situation has changed since the height of the activities of the *Psichiatria Democratica*; after the decline of the influence of the Communist Party, which supported these developments, some of its programme has been hijacked by the new right-wing ideology.

6 This has been pointed out by Treacher and Baruch in *Critical Psychiatry* (Teacher and Baruch 1981:147).

7 Laing never referred to their work in his writings and in a late interview he was dismissive of them (Mullan 1995:209–212).

8 Anna O., Augustine and Dora were just as different from each other as Mary Barnes was different from them. Augustine escaped from the hospital when she was sixteen and nothing is known of her subsequent life; Anna O. was in real life Bertha Pappenheim and after her treatment with Breuer she acquired nationwide prominence for her fight for women's rights and for her pioneering social work; Dora, by all accounts, remained throughout her life a psychological wreck.

9 See for example Wing (1978:162).

10 La Borde has been an influential anti-psychiatric project in France. Like Villa 21 it is a ward in a larger hospital.

11 Laing gave his own account of the story (Mullan 1995:323–325). It does not differ in any essential from the book.

12 A recent publication presents the work of The Arbours Association, including the activities in the households (Berke *et al.* eds. 1995).

13 Gilles Deleuze and Félix Guattari in their *Anti-Oedipus* also produced a vision of madness as a revolutionary force which refuses fixity and definition and allows one to escape the Oedipal cycle of familiality. They, in fact, use the term 'schizophrenia' (and have invented the term schizoanalysis) for this force and oppose it to the paranoid-capitalist state of our normality. Their notion of schizophrenia, it has to be added, is a literary invention which has little in common with the states of mind psychiatrists designate as schizophrenia (Deleuze and Guattari 1984).

14 Jervis's excellent analysis of this problem is addressed mostly to the views of Deleuze and Guattari in *Anti-Oedipus* but is just as applicable to Cooper. Interestingly Cooper reproaches Jervis for not taking seriously the revolutionary potential of madness (Cooper 1980:145).

15 *Asylum* has been the most consistent outlet where the views of the patients are expressed. The figure behind the magazine is Alec Jenner, Professor Emeritus of the University of Sheffield, former director of the Medical Research Council for metabolic studies in psychiatry. He has been one of the initiators of *Asylum*, and has virtually run it. Professor Jenner merits particular mention because he seems to be the only senior psychiatrist in the UK who takes seriously the question of patients' rights.

Chronology

1927	Born 7 October in Glasgow. The only child of lower-middle-class Presbyterian parents. Primary and Grammar School in Glasgow
1945	Goes to Glasgow University to study medicine.
1951	Graduates from medical school and after six months of a neurological internship is drafted to the Army Psychiatric Hospital.
1953	Leaves the army and begins work at Glasgow Royal Mental Hospital.
1955	Appointed senior registrar at Glasgow University Psychiatry Clinic. Publishes (with Cameron and McGhie) paper, 'Patient and Nurse Effects of Environmental Changes in the Care of Chronic Schizophrenics'.
1957	Moves to London where he takes up a post at the Tavistock Family Research Programme. Begins psychoanalytical training.
1958	Publishes (with Esterson) paper, 'The Collusive Function of Pairing in Analytic Groups'.
1960	Publication of *The Divided Self*.
1961	Moves to Tavistock Institute. Publication of *Self and Others*.
1962	Becomes director of the Langham Clinic.
1964	Publishes (with Cooper) *Reason and Violence. A Decade of Sartre's Philosophy. 1950–1960* and (with Esterson) *Sanity, Madness and the Family*.
1965	The Philadelphia Association founded. Moves into the Kingsley Hall therapeutic community. Leaves the Langham Clinic.

1966	Publishes (with Phillipson and Lee) *Interpersonal Perception*. Moves out of Kingsley Hall.
1967	Publishes *The Politics of Experience* and *The Bird of Paradise*. Leaves the Tavistock Institute. Forms Institute of Phenomenological Studies with David Cooper, John Heaten and others. Participates in the organization and running of the Dialectics of Liberation Conference in London.
1968	Paper, 'Metanoia: Some Experiences at Kingsley Hall', published. 'The Obvious', Laing's address to the Conference on the Dialectics of Liberation, published.
1969	*The Politics of the Family* published in Canada.
1970	Kingsley Hall closes down. *Knots* published.
1971–2	Away in Ceylon (now Sri Lanka) and India.
1973	Publishes in England *The Politics of the Family and Other Essays*.
1976	Publishes 'A Critique of Kallmann's and Slater's Genetic Theory of Schizophrenia', a paper written some fifteen years earlier.
1976	Publishes *The Facts of Life*.
1976	Publishes *Do You Love Me?*
1977	Publishes *Conversations with Children*.
1979	Publishes *Sonnets*.
1982	Publishes *The Voice of Experience. Experience, Science and Psychiatry*.
1985	Publishes *Wisdom, Madness and Folly. The Making of a Psychiatrist*. Resigns from the medical register of the General Medical Council.
1989	23 August, Laing died of a heart attack on a tennis court in St Tropez.

Laing married three times and had ten children.

Bibliography

Artaud, A. (1976) 'Van Gogh, The Man Suicided by Society' in S. Sontag (ed.) *Selected Writings*, Berkeley, Los Angeles: University of California Press.

Barnes, M. (1989) (with Scott, A.) *Something Sacred: Conversations, Writings, Paintings*, London: Free Association Books.

Barnes, M. and Berke, J. (1973) *Mary Barnes. Two Accounts of a Journey Through Madness*, Harmondsworth: Penguin Books.

Basaglia, F. (ed.) (1968) *L'Istituzione Negata*, Torino: Einaudi, tr. as (1970) *L'Institution en Négation*, Paris: Seuil.

—— (ed.) (1973) *Che cos'è la Psichiatria?*, Torino: Einaudi; tr. as (1977) *Qu'est-ce que la Psychiatrie?*, Paris: Presses Universitaires de France.

—— (1981) 'Breaking the Circuit of Control' in D. Ingleby (ed.) *Critical Psychiatry*, Harmondsworth: Penguin Books.

Bateson, G., Haley, J., Jackson, D. and Weakland, J. (1956) 'Towards a Theory of Schizophrenia' in G. Bateson (ed.) (1973) *Steps to an Ecology of Mind*, St Albans: Granada Publishing Limited.

Bateson, G. (ed.) (1973) *Steps to an Ecology of Mind*, St Albans: Granada.

—— (ed.) (1974) [1961] *Perceval's Narrative. A Patient's Account of his Psychosis, 1830–1832*, New York: William Morrow.

Berke, J.H. (1979) *I Haven't Had to Go Mad Here*, Harmondsworth: Penguin Books.

Berke, J.H., Masoliver, C. and Ryan, T.J. (eds) (1995) *Sanctuary*, London: Process Press.

Binswanger, L. (1963) *Being in the World*, New York: Basic Books.

Bleuler, E. (1950) *Dementia Praecox or the Group of Schizophrenias*, New York: International Universities Press.

Boyers, R. and Orrill, R. (eds) (1972) *Laing and Anti-Psychiatry*, Harmondsworth: Penguin Books.

Britton, D. (1974) 'Laing's Social Philosophy' in *Radical Philosophy* 7, pp. 29–30.

Bullard, D.M. (ed.) (1959) *Psychoanalysis and Psychotherapy. Selected Papers of Frieda Fromm-Reichmann*, Chicago: The University of Chicago Press.

Clare, A. (1992) *In the Psychiatrist's Chair*, London: Heinemann.

Claridge, G. (1990) 'Can a Disease Model of Schizophrenia Survive?' in R.P. Bental (ed.) *Reconstructing Schizophrenia*, London: Routledge.

Coate, Morag (1964) *Beyond all Reason*, London: Constable.

Collier, A. (1977) *R.D. Laing: The Philosophy and Politics of Psychotherapy,* New York: Pantheon Books.

Coltart, N. (1995) 'Attention' in J.H. Berke, C. Masoliver and T.J. Ryan (eds) *Sanctuary,* London: Process Press.

Cooper, D. (1967) *Psychiatry and Anti-Psychiatry,* London: Tavistock.

—— (ed.) (1968) *The Dialectics of Liberation,* Harmondsworth: Penguin Books.

—— (1980) *The Language of Madness,* Harmondsworth: Penguin Books.

Deleuze, G. and Guattari, F. (1984) *Anti-Oedipus,* trans. R. Hurley, M. Seem, and H.R. Lane, London: The Athlone Press.

Donnelly, M. (1992) *The Politics of Mental Health in Italy,* London: Routledge.

Donzelot, J. (1979) *The Policing of Families,* trans. R. Hurley, London: Hutchinson.

Esterson, A. (1972) *The Leaves of Spring,* Harmondsworth: Penguin Books.

Evans, R. (ed.) (1976) *R.D. Laing. The Man and his Ideas,* New York: E.P. Dutton.

Fanon, F. (1965) *The Wretched of the Earth,* London: MacGibbon and Kee.

Federn, P. (1977) *Ego Psychology and the Psychoses,* London: Maresfield Reprints.

Foucault, M. (1971) *Madness and Civilization,* London: Tavistock.

Friedenberg, E.Z. (1973) *Laing,* London: Fontana.

Goffman, E. (1970) *Asylums. Essays on the Social Situation of Mental Patients and Other Inmates,* Harmondsworth: Penguin Books.

Guattari, F. (1984) 'Mary Barnes or Oedipus in Anti-Psychiatry', trans. R. Sheed, in *Molecular Revolution. Psychiatry and Politics,* Harmondsworth: Penguin Books.

Heidegger, M. (1962) *Being and Time,* trans. J. Macquarrie and E. Robinson, Oxford: Blackwell.

Henry, J. (1962) *Culture Against Man,* Harmondsworth: Penguin Books.

Howarth-Williams, M. (1977) *R.D. Laing: His Work and its Relevance for Sociology,* London: Routledge & Kegan Paul.

Hunter, R. and Macalpine, I. (1963) *Three Hundred Years of Psychiatry (1535–1860),* London: Oxford University Press.

Ingleby, D. (ed.) (1981) *Critical Psychiatry: The Politics of the Mental State,* Harmondsworth: Penguin Books.

Isaacs, S. (1952) 'The Nature and Function of Phantasy' in J. Rivière (ed.) *Developments in Psycho-Analysis,* London: Hogarth.

Jacoby, R. (1975) *Social Amnesia: A Critique of Conformist Psychology from Adler to Laing,* Boston, MA: Beacon Press.

Jaspers, K. (1962) *General Psychopathology,* Manchester: Manchester University Press.

Jervis, G. (1967) 'Psychiatrists and Politics' in M. Donnelly (1992) *The Politics of Mental Health in Italy,* London: Routledge.

Jervis, G. (1977) *Le Mythe de l'Antipsychiatrie,* Paris: Solin.

Kaplan, B. (ed.) (1964) *The Inner World of Mental Illness,* New York and London: Harper and Row.

Kierkegaard, S. (1954) *The Sickness unto Death,* trans. H. Lowrie, New York: Doubleday.

Kotowicz, Z. (1993) 'Tradition, Violence and Psychotherapy' in L. Spurling (ed.) *From the Words of my Mouth. Tradition and Psychotherapy*, London: Routledge.

Kraepelin, E. (1905) *Lectures on Clinical Psychiatry*, London: Baillière, Tindall & Cox.

Laing, A. (1994) *R.D. Laing. A Biography*, London: Peter Owen Publishers.

Laing, R.D. (1955) (with Cameron, J.L. and McGhie, A.) 'Patient and Nurse Effects of Environmental Changes in the Care of Chronic Schizophrenics', *The Lancet*, vol. 2, pp. 1384–86.

—— (1958) (with Esterson, A.) 'The Collusive Function of Pairing in Analytic Groups', *British Journal of Medical Psychology* 31, pp. 117–23.

—— (1962) 'Series and Nexus in the Family', *New Left Review* 15, May–June.

—— (1964) [1960] *The Divided Self*, Harmondsworth: Penguin Books.

—— (1966) [1961] *Self and Others*, Harmondsworth: Penguin Books.

—— (1964) (with Cooper, D.) *Reason and Violence. A Decade of Sartre's Philosophy. 1950–1960*, London: Tavistock.

—— (1967) [1964] (with Esterson, A.) *Sanity, Madness and the Family*, Harmondsworth: Penguin Books.

—— (1965) (with Esterson, A. and Cooper, D.) 'Results of Family-Oriented Therapy with Hospitalized Schizophrenics', *British Medical Journal* 2, December, pp. 1462–5.

—— (1966) (with Phillipson, H. and Lee, A.R.) *Interpersonal Perception*, London: Tavistock.

—— (1967) *The Politics of Experience* and *The Bird of Paradise*, Harmondsworth: Penguin Books.

—— (1968) 'Metanoia: Some Experiences at Kingsley Hall', *Recherches*, Paris, December. (Reprinted in H.W. Ruitenbeek (ed.) (1972) *Going Crazy*, New York: Bantam Books.)

—— (1968) 'The Obvious' in D. Cooper (ed.) *The Dialectics of Liberation*, Harmondsworth: Penguin Books.

—— (1969) *The Politics of the Family*, Toronto: CBC Publications.

—— (1970) *Knots*, Harmondsworth: Penguin Books.

—— (1976) [1973] *The Politics of the Family and Other Essays*, Harmondsworth: Penguin Books.

—— (1976) 'A Critique of Kallmann's and Slater's Genetic Theory of Schizophrenia' in R. Evans (ed.) *R.D. Laing. The Man and his Ideas*, New York: E.P. Dutton.

—— (1976) *The Facts of Life*, Harmondsworth: Penguin Books.

—— (1976) *Do You Love Me?* Harmondsworth: Penguin Books.

—— (1977) *Conversations with Children*, Harmondsworth: Penguin Books.

—— (1979) *Sonnets*, London: Michael Joseph.

—— (1982) *The Voice of Experience. Experience, Science and Psychiatry*, London: Allen Lane.

—— (1985) *Wisdom, Madness and Folly. The Making of a Psychiatrist*, London: Macmillan.

Laplanche, J. and Pontalis, J.-B. (1980) *The Language of Psychoanalysis*, London: Hogarth Press.

Mannoni, M. (1970) *The Child, His 'Illness', and the Others*, London: Tavistock.

Marcuse, H. (1964) *One-Dimensional Man*, London: Routledge & Kegan Paul.

May, R., Angel, E. and Ellenberger, H.F. (1958) *Existence – A New Dimension in Psychiatry and Psychology*, New York: Touchstone Books.

Merleau-Ponty, M. (1962) *The Phenomenology of Perception*, London: Routledge & Kegan Paul.

Mezan, P. (1972) 'After Freud and Jung, Now Comes R.D. Laing Pop-Shrink Rebel, Yogi, Philosopher King, Latest Reincarnation of Aesculapius, Maybe', *Esquire*, January: 92–97, 160–78.

Minkowski, E. (1970) *Lived Time*, Chicago: Northwestern University Press.

Mitchell, J. (1974) *Psychoanalysis and Feminism*, Harmondsworth: Penguin Books.

Mullan, B. (1995) *Mad to be Normal. Conversations with R.D. Laing*, London: Free Association Books.

Pankow, G. (1983) *Structure Familiale et Psychose*, Paris: Aubier.

Reed, D. (1979) *Anna*, Harmondsworth: Penguin Books.

Rosen, J.N. (1962) *Direct Psychoanalytic Psychiatry*, New York: Grune & Stratton.

Rosenham, D.L. (1975) 'On Being Sane in Insane Places' in T.J. Scheff (ed.) *Labeling Madness*, New Jersey: Prentice Hall.

Roustang, F. (1982) *Dire Mastery*, Baltimore, MD.: Johns Hopkins University Press.

Ruitenbeek, H.W. (ed.) (1972) *Going Crazy*, New York: Bantam Books.

Sartre, J.-P. (1961) *Critique de la Raison Dialectique*, Paris: Gallimard.

Sartre, J.-P. (1962) *Being and Nothingness*, trans. H. Barnes, London: Methuen.

Scull, A.T. (ed.) (1981) *Madhouses, Mad-Doctors and Madmen: The Social History of Psychiatry in the Victorian Era*, London: Athlone Press.

—— (1982) *Museums of Madness: The Social Organization of Insanity in Nineteenth Century England*, Harmondsworth: Penguin Books.

Searles, H. (1965) *Collected Papers on Schizophrenia and Related Subjects*, New York: International Universities Press.

Sedgwick, P. (1972) 'R.D. Laing: Self, Symptom and Society' in R. Boyers and R. Orrill (eds) *Laing and Anti-Psychiatry*, Harmondsworth: Penguin Books.

—— (1982) *Psycho Politics*, London: Pluto Press.

Showalter, E. (1987) *The Female Malady: Women, Madness and English Culture, 1830–1980*, London: Virago Press.

Siegler, M., Osmond, H. and Mann, H. (1972) 'Laing's Models of Madness' in R. Boyers and R. Orrill (eds) *Laing and Anti-Psychiatry*, Harmondsworth: Penguin Books.

Sigal, C. (1976) *Zone of the Interior*, New York: Thomas Y. Crowell.

Skultans, V. (1975) *Madness and Morals: Ideas on Insanity in the Nineteenth Century*, London: Routledge & Kegan Paul.

SPK (Sozialistisches Patienten Kollektiv) (1972) *Psychiatrie Politique*, Paris: François Maspero.

—— (1973) *Faire de la Maladie une Arme*, Paris: Editions Champ Libre.

Sullivan, H.S. (1953) *Conceptions of Modern Psychiatry*, New York: Norton.

Szasz, T.S. (1972) *The Myth of Mental Illness*, St Albans: Granada.

—— (1973) *The Manufacture of Madness*, St Albans: Granada.

—— (ed.) (1974) *The Age of Madness*, London: Routledge & Kegan Paul.

—— (1976) 'Anti-Psychiatry: The Paradigm of a Plundered Mind' in *New Review* 3(29) (off-print).

Tillich, P. (1952) *The Courage to Be*, London: Nisbet.

Treacher, A. and Baruch, G. (1981) 'Towards a Critical History of the Psychiatric Profession' in D. Ingleby (ed.) *Critical Psychiatry*, Harmondsworth: Penguin Books.

Turkle, S. (1979) *Psychoanalytic Politics. Freud's French Revolution*, London: Burnett Books.

Wing, J.K. (1978) *Reasoning About Madness*, Oxford: Oxford University Press.

Winnicott, D.W. (1960) 'Ego Distortion in Terms of True–False Self' in *The Maturational Processes and the Facilitating Environment* [1979], London: Hogarth.

—— (1982) *Playing and Reality*, Harmondsworth: Penguin Books.

Index